BOOST YOUR

VOCABULARY 4

Chris Barker

PENGUIN ENGLISH GUIDES

Pearson Education Limited
Edinburgh Gate
Harlow
Essex CM20 2JE, England
and Associated Companies throughout the world.

ISBN 0582 451655

First published 2002
Copyright © Chris Barker 2002

1 3 5 7 9 10 8 6 4 2

Design and typesetting by Mackerel Limited
Illustrations by Mark Davis
Printed in Spain by Cayfosa-Quebecor, Barcelona

Acknowledgements

With thanks to Helen Parker of Penguin Longman Publishing, for helping to shape the material and for her encouragement during the writing process; to Theresa Clementson, whose good sense, good humour and hard work made the transition from typescript to printed page seem effortless; and to Diane Winkleby, who opened my eyes to some of the delights of American English.

Chris Barker
London, 2002

The publishers make grateful acknowledgement for permission to reproduce the following copyright material:

Capital Pictures, pages 10,46; Dorling Kindersley/I. Beckman, page 28, /P. Gatward /J. Heseltine, page 73; Hulton Deutsch Collection/Corbis, pages 41, 52; Granada Visual, page 52; Camera Press/M. Argyles, page 52; Gettyimages, /Doug Menuez, page 52, /Steve Campbell, /Bobbi Tull, page 73, Eyewire, pages 23, 28, 41, 52, 62, 63; The Independent/John Voos, page 62; Allstar, page 61; National Gallery of Art, Washington DC, USA/Bridgeman Art Library, page 74; Digitalvision, page 80

Every effort has been made to trace copyright holders in every case. The publishers would be interested to hear from any not acknowledged here.

Published by Pearson Education Limited in association with Penguin Books Ltd, both companies being subsidiaries of Pearson plc.

For a complete list of the titles available from Penguin English please write to your local Pearson Education office or to: Marketing Department, Penguin Longman Publishing, 80 Strand, London WC2R ORL.

Contents

Introduction

Expanding your vocabulary

At the intermediate and upper-intermediate stages of language learning, the vocabulary you need is wide-ranging and varied. You already have a good knowledge of the words and phrases which frequently occur in common topic areas. The aim of this book is to widen and deepen your knowledge. It will help you to understand and express more complex ideas concerning people and relationships, politics, the environment and crime; to deal with a variety of situations, from describing what is wrong with a piece of equipment to arranging a working holiday; and to talk about areas of general interest, such as the media, books and art.

Boost Your Vocabulary 4 is divided into twelve topic areas, with important words and phrases listed within specific contexts. The topic area in Unit 1, for example, is *People and relationships*. Vocabulary is presented in the contexts of *Relating to other people* (e.g. *outgoing / shy, reserved*), *Friendship and relationships* (e.g. *best friend* and *acquaintance*, *be keen on* and *go out with*), and *Life stages* (e.g. *be brought up by ...* , *leave home* and *move house*). The exercises which follow start by focusing on single words and then build towards longer writing activities, with opportunities to express aspects of your own experience. At the end of each unit you can list words and expressions which you want to memorize.

How to use *Boost Your Vocabulary 4*

Working on your own or in class, you can use this book in three ways:

1 To practise and learn more vocabulary

- Choose a topic area of interest to you.
- Read the lists of words and phrases in the topic area.
- Translate the words and phrases into your language in the spaces provided, using a good bilingual dictionary.
- Remember to look at the context of the words and phrases when translating them. If an exact equivalent does not exist (e.g. for words to do with the law, such as *solicitor*) you may need to use a symbol such as ≈ to mean *approximately equivalent to*. You will find 'help' boxes on the page to guide you.
- Do the practice exercises. Try not to refer to the vocabulary lists when you are writing.

- Check your work by looking back at the vocabulary lists.
- Finally, use the Answer key to mark and correct your work.

2 To help you with written and spoken work

- When you are working on a particular topic in class, use the lists to help you with writing or speaking.

- Do the practice exercises at home to help you use the words and phrases in a variety of contexts.

3 To revise before a test

- Test yourself on particular topics by looking at your translations and giving the English words or phrases.
- Try this on your own and with a partner.

Types of exercise

There are word puzzles, quizzes, surveys and questionnaires; there are exercises which ask you to organize words into groups; and there are opportunities for continuous writing. The aim of all of the exercises is to help you remember vocabulary and use it correctly.

Symbols

Some of the exercises have symbols, to help you identify them quickly:

 spelling

 word groups

 memorization

 When you see this symbol, you should write in your notebook.

Answer key

The answers to the exercises and the tests are in a special pull-out section in the centre of the book.

Tests

There are tests after Units 4, 8 and 12. They revise the language of Units 1 to 4, 5 to 8 and 9 to 12. They will help you to see how well you are doing.

Reference

When you see this symbol you can find more information in the reference section at the back of the book. It includes a unit-by-unit list comparing British and American English spelling (e.g. *fibre / fiber*) and vocabulary (e.g. *get on with someone / get along with someone*). Boxes showing this symbol will also refer you to other relevant parts of the book, and to relevant sections in *Boost Your Vocabulary 1, 2* and *3*.

Self assessment and progress checks

On page 88 you will find charts which will help you to assess and record how much progress you are making.

1 People and relationships

REF See also **Boost Your Vocabulary 3**, pages 6 – 7, (People).

Translate the words and phrases.

Relating to other people

Adjectives		Opposites	
outgoing	....	shy, reserved	....
talkative	....	quiet	....
frank	....	secretive	....
self-confident	....	unsure (of yourself)	....
affectionate, warm	....	cold	....
submissive	....	bossy*	....
meek	....	aggressive	....
kind	....	malicious, spiteful, mean	....
straight	....	two-faced*	....
popular	....	unpopular	....
sympathetic	....	unsympathetic	....
helpful	....	unhelpful	....
trustworthy	....	untrustworthy	....
trusting	....	cynical	....
sociable	....	unsociable	....
romantic	....	unromantic	....
self-conscious	....	unselfconscious	....
faithful	....	unfaithful	....
dependent	....	independent	....
considerate	....	inconsiderate	....
		possessive	....
		competitive	....

*Adjectives marked * are used in conversational, informal language.*

Verbs and verb phrases

respect	....
admire	....
fancy	....
adore	....
like	....
dislike	....
hate	....
can't stand	....

It was love at first sight.

get on with (= be friendly with) ....

fall out with (= stop being friendly with) ....

stand up for (= support or defend) ....

look up to (= admire) ....

look down on (= think you are better than) ....

Friendship and relationships

best friend ....

close friend ....

acquaintance ....

boyfriend / girlfriend ....

partner ....

fiancé (male) ....

fiancée (female) ....

husband ....

wife ....

single parent ....

(get / be) engaged ....

engagement ....

(get / be) married ....

marriage ....

(get / be) divorced ....

divorce ....

(be) separated ....

separation ....

be keen on ....

be attracted to ....

fancy ....

flirt (with) ....

fall in love (with) ....

be in love (with) ....

go out (with) ....

split up (with) ....

break up (with) ....

make up (with) ....

Are you in a relationship at the moment?

....

It was love at first sight.

....

They drifted apart.

....

Life stages

be born in (place) in (year)

....

be brought up by

....

be educated at ... school

....

go to college ....

leave home ....

start work ....

get a job ....

get married ....

have children ....

move house ....

retire ....

die ....

REF *See page 86 for the British / American word list.*

1

abc **1** The pairs of words have similar meanings. Complete them.

1 kind   con _s i d e r a t e_
2 loyal   fai _ _ _ _ _
3 friendly   soc _ _ _ _ _
4 honest   tru _ _ _ _ _ _ _ _
5 extrovert   out _ _ _ _ _

6 open   fra _ _
7 nasty   spi _ _ _ _ _
8 insincere   two- _ _ _ _ _
9 insecure   uns _ _ _
10 weak   sub _ _ _ _ _ _ _

2 Write these adjectives in groups.

affectionate   self-confident   assertive   unsociable   inconsiderate
aggressive   romantic   dependent   unromantic   competitive
talkative   faithful   reserved   unselfconscious helpful

good	bad	sometimes good, sometimes bad
....	....	....
....	....	....
....	....	....
....	....	....
....	....	....
....	....	....

If you are working in class, compare your answers with a partner or group.

3 Use the words in the box to describe these people.

possessive	independent	cold	sympathetic	secretive
malicious	meek	quiet	bossy	popular

1 You never really know what she's thinking.   _secretive_
2 He's always saying nasty things about people.   ....
3 He's a really nice guy, but he won't stand up for himself.   ....
4 She gets invited to lots of parties.   ....
5 He's quite old now, but he still likes to do everything for himself. ....
6 She's always telling people what to do.   ....
7 He understands people really well and sees things from
   their point of view.   ....
8 She gets really annoyed if another girl talks to him at a party.   ....
9 He just sits there and doesn't say anything.   ....
10 She's not a warm, affectionate person.   ....

4a Use a verb (in the correct tense) and a preposition from each column to complete the sentences.

verb +	preposition 1 +	preposition 2
get	up	with
look	out	for
look	out	with
stand	on	to
fall	up	on
break	down	with
go	up	with

1 They used to be good friends, but then he .....*fell out with*............. her parents and they don't speak now.

2 He's a very sociable person. He .... everybody.

3 They're boyfriend and girlfriend. He .... her for ages.

4 They had an argument, and the relationship is over. She .... him last weekend.

5 Why are you so arrogant? You just .... everybody.

6 Don't worry about being bullied. I .... you.

7 Footballers are heroes for some kids. My son really .... them.

4b Choose a sentence from 4a to describe these situations.

Sentence ..*2*..

Sentence .....

Sentence .....

Sentence .....

1

5   Complete the questionnaire.

Find out how YOU relate to people.

1 Do you ever flirt? (Be honest!)

a Sometimes
b No, never
c All the time

4 Which of these people do you most admire?

a Madonna
b David Beckham
c Mahatma Gandhi

2 How many close friends have you got?

a More than ten
b Between three and ten
c Fewer than three

5 In a group, are you the one who ...

a talks least?
b talks most?
c tries to include everybody in the conversation?

3 Have you ever fallen in love?

a Yes, I have.
b I might have done but I'm not telling you.
c Listen, I fall in love at least twice a week.

6 If you're attracted to someone, do you...

a go up to them and say, 'I really fancy you'?
b ask a friend for their telephone number?
c run away?

Check your score and read the analysis on page A.

6a   Complete what A, B and C say about themselves.

Person A	
I'll ..*fall in love*... with a fantastically rich, good-looking boy / girl. It'll .... We'll .... soon afterwards. We'll .... before I'm 25. We'll .... at least three children, a big house and lots of parties.	have fall in love get engaged be love at first sight get married

Person B	
I'll .... a few people before I find the right one. We'll tell each other everything. We'll probably .... till we .... but if we .... we'll always be good friends.	die break up go out with stay together

Person C	
I .... in love. I don't know whether I'll meet anyone. I won't .... Just think, your partner might turn out to be a real pain, although I suppose you can always .... Anyway, I .... long relationships.	can't stand don't believe marry get divorced

6b Use two adjectives from the box to describe each person.

cold	faithful	cynical	Person A	....
romantic	trusting	sociable	Person B	....
			Person C	....

6c Write a short paragraph about what you think the future holds for you. (Use 6a as a model.)

7 Number these sentences in a logical sequence. Then write about an older person you know.

☐ She and her husband moved house in 1978.

☐ She died in 2001.

☐ She got married in 1946 and had two children.

☐ She was brought up by her grandparents.

☐ She retired in 1977.

☐ She went to college, but she still lived at home.

[1] She was born in London in 1917.

☐ She left home when she was 18.

☐ She was educated at the local grammar school.

☐ She started work at an engineering firm in 1938.

8 Write ten words and five expressions you are going to memorize.

Words	Expressions
1	1 ....
2	....
3	2 ....
4	....
5	3 ....
6	....
7	4 ....
8	....
9	5 ....
10	....

2 Everyday life

Translate the words and phrases.

Around the house

a pane of glass

....

a sliver of glass

....

a sheet of paper

....

a scrap of paper

....

a block of wood / ice

....

a splinter of wood

....

a speck of dust

....

a bar of soap

....

a blade of grass

....

a wisp of smoke

....

a pile of newspapers

....

a stack of books

....

a heap of rubbish

....

a bundle of old clothes

....

REF See also **Boost Your Vocabulary 2**, page 18 (Quantities).

Food

a piece of cheese

....

a joint of meat

....

a slice of cake

....

a bar of chocolate

....

a segment of orange

....

a lump of butter

....

a drop of milk

....

a pinch of salt

....

a squeeze of lemon juice

....

a grain of rice

....

a bunch of grapes

....

sugar cubes / lumps

....

ice cubes

....

breadcrumbs

....

Would you like a squeeze of lemon? Yes, please.

And would you like some on your fish as well?

See page 86 for the British / American word list.

Problems

It's not working. / It's broken.

....

There's something wrong with the TV.

....

What a mess!

....

It has shrunk.

....

It's (It is + *adjective*) ...		There's (There is + *noun*) ...	
1	blocked	a blockage	....
2	dented	a dent	....
3	stained	a stain	....
4	ripped	a rip	....
5	flooded	a flood	....
6	leaking	a leak	....
7	torn	a tear	....
8	damaged		
9	stuck		
10	burnt		
11	smashed		

Solutions

Get it mended / repaired / replaced.

....

Get someone to look at it.

....

Throw it away.

....

Clean it up.

....

Everyday sounds (verbs and nouns)

ring	....	whirr	....
crash	....	buzz	....
crunch	....	rustle	....
pop	....	jingle	....
crack	....	snap	....
crackle	....	splash	....
fizz	....	tick	....
hiss	....		

2

1a Match the units with the food.

Units		Food	
1	a slice of	a	butter
2	a bar of	b	cake
3	a bunch of	c	lemon juice
4	a squeeze of	d	chocolate
5	a pinch of	e	grapes
6	a joint of	f	meat
7	a lump of	g	milk
8	a grain of	h	orange
9	a segment of	i	rice
10	a drop of	j	salt

1 b *a slice of cake* .... ☐
2 ☐ .... ☐
3 ☐ .... ☐
4 ☐ .... ☐
5 ☐ .... ☐
6 ☐ .... ☐
7 ☐ .... ☐
8 ☐ .... ☐
9 ☐ .... ☐
10 ☐ .... ☐

1b Tick the ones you have had in the last 24 hours.

2a Replace the words in colour with a more specific word.

1 We need a new piece of soap in the bathroom.   *bar* ....

2 You broke the window, so you'll have to pay
   for a new piece of glass.   ....

3 I cut my finger on a small sharp piece of glass.   ....

4 Use a fresh piece of paper.   ....

5 I only need a small piece of paper.   ....

6 Your house is so clean. There isn't a tiny piece of dust anywhere. ....

7 A tiny piece of wood went into my hand.   ....

8 Can you hold a piece of grass between your thumbs
   and blow on it to make a noise?   ....

9 My feet are so cold. They're like large pieces of ice! ....

2b Complete the sentences. Don't use the same word more than once.

1 A thin *wisp*..................... of smoke rose from the chimney of the cottage.

2 What do you want with that .... of old newspapers?

3 I've got a .... of books to read before term starts.

4 What's that .... of rubbish in the corner? Put it in the bin!

5 I'll tie these old clothes into a .... and you can take them to the
   charity shop.

2c List the things in 2a and 2b that you can see now.

a pane of glass, ...

3a Describe the problems using a different expression each time.

1 The on / off switch on my computer *is stuck*.

2 The toast ....

3 The window ....

4 There's a .... on my shirt.

5 The pockets ....

6 The fan ....

7 The side of the car ....

8 My pen ....

3b Match the solutions to the problems in 3a.

> **Solutions**
>
> ● Take it to the dry cleaner's.
>
> ● You'll have to get them mended.
>
> ● Throw it away and start again.
>
> ● You'll have to get someone to look at it and tell you how much the repair will cost.
>
> ● Buy a new one.
>
> ● You'll have to take it back to the shop.
>
> ● You'll have to get it replaced.
>
> ● You'll have to call the engineer.

1 *You'll have to call the engineer.*

2 ....

3 ....

4 ....

5 ....

6 ....

7 ....

8 ....

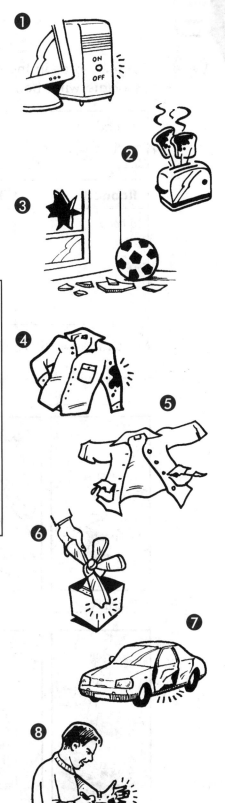

4 Put the words in the correct column according to the problems which you associate with them.

| a road | a sink | a toilet | a bank note |
| a piece of paper | a jumper | a kitchen | a computer image |

flooded	**torn**	**blocked**	**shrunk**
a road		*a road*	

5 Match the words to the pictures.

| buzz | crackle | fizz | ring | splash |
| crack | crash | pop | rustle | tick |

1 .....*crack*..... 2 .... 3 .... 4 .... 5 ....

6................. 7 .... 8 .... 9 .... 10 ....

6a Use the words in the box to complete the opening of this short story. (Change the form where necessary.)

| jingle | whirr | hiss | snap | crunch |

Their footsteps [1] _crunched_ on the gravel as they approached the house. The man's keys [2] .... in his pocket. He took his sunglasses out and [3] .... the case shut.

"Be quiet!" the woman [4] .... through her teeth. They could hear the [5] .... of helicopter blades in the distance.

6b Write the next paragraph of the story using some of the words in 3a, 4, 5 and 6a.

....
....
....
....
....
....
....
....

7 Write ten words and five expressions you are going to memorize.

Words	Expressions
1	1 ....
2	
3	2 ....
4	
5	3 ....
6	
7	4 ....
8	
9	5 ....
10	

3 The business world

Translate the words and phrases.

Work places

office	....	factory	....
head office	....	industrial estate	....

People at work

employer	....	boss*	....
employee	....	sales team	....
MD (managing director)	....	sales representative (rep*)	....
finance director	....	workmate (in a factory)	....
sales director	....		
marketing director	....	colleague (in an office)	....
(line) manager	....		

> A **line manager** is someone who is one level higher than you and is in charge of your work.

> Words marked * are used in informal, conversational language.

member of a trade union

....

union representative

....

Company departments

human resources	....
marketing	....
production	....
sales	....
distribution	....
accounts	....
admin(istration)	....
technical support	....

The working day

have ...

an early start	....
a meeting	....
an appointment	....
a conference	....
a coffee break	....
a lunch break	....
a working lunch	....

Self-employment

I work from home.

....

I'm self-employed.

....

I'm a self-employed builder.

....

I'm a freelance graphic designer.

....

> Use **self-employed** for people who do not work for a company but who do practical jobs like building and plumbing; use **freelance** for people who work independently for several companies or organizations, e.g. freelance journalists, freelance photographers.

Finding and getting a job

job advertisement /
advert / ad
....

vacancy
....

application form
....

referee
....

reference
....

job description
....

duties
....

relevant experience
....

I'd like to apply (for the job).

....

When are you available for interview?

....

 REF

See page 84 for a list of jobs. See also **Boost Your Vocabulary 3**, page 39.

Use **firm** when you are talking about providing a service and **company** when you are talking about producing goods.

Pay, responsibilities and promotion

I get a bonus.
....

I work on commission.
....

I'm in charge of the company budget.
....

What are the prospects for promotion?
....

I've been promoted to senior manager.
....

Types of work

What does she do for a living?
....

She's a dentist.
....

He's in the army.
....

She works as a secretary in a school.
....

He works in / He's in | insurance.
| the textile industry.

....

....

She works for | an oil company.
| a law firm.

....

....

He works at the local supermarket.
....

Problems

She was fired.
....

He was sacked. / He got the sack.*
....

She was made redundant.
....

He lost his job.
....

She's out of work.
....

He's unemployed.
....

They've gone on strike.
....

And what sort of job do you want, Miss Bradshaw?

CAREERS OFFICE

 REF

A well-paid one.

See page 86 for the British / American word list.

3

abc ✓ **1a** Complete the diagram showing the company structure.

man..*aging*... director

fin............. director   sa.......... director   mark.............. director

acc............ manager   hum........ res............ manager   prod............. manager

sales rep..................   tech............. support staff   ad........................ staff

1b Match what these people say to one of the jobs in 1a.

1   My responsibility, quite simply, is the whole company! *the managing director* ....

2   I'm in charge of making the things we sell. ....

3   I'm in charge of the company budget. ....

4   I'm in charge of advertising and promotion. ....

5   I'm in charge of the sales team. ....

6   I have to make sure that the bills and wages are paid. ....

7   We're part of a team. Our job is to find customers and sell to them. ....

8   My job is to recruit people and sort out any problems people may have. ....

9   We organize company travel. ....

10 If you've got a problem with your computer, just call us! ....

2a Match the words in the columns to make phrases.

1	a freelance	a	commission	1	..c..	*a freelance editor*	
2	a law	b	director	2	......	....	
3	a managing	c	editor	3	......	....	
4	a self-employed	d	firm	4	......	....	
5	admin	e	job	5	......	....	
6	a union	f	plumber	6	......	....	
7	a well-paid	g	redundant	7	......	....	
8	to be made	h	representative	8	......	....	
9	to go on	i	staff	9	......	....	
10	to work on	j	strike	10	......	....	

2b Write three true sentences about yourself or people you know, using the phrases in 2a.

My friend Jorge has a very well-paid job. I would never go on strike.

1 ....

2 ....

3 ....

3 Solve the crossword.

Across ➤

1 When are you … for interview? (9)

5 As we're busy, let's … a working lunch. (4)

6 Traditionally, businessmen wore black or … suits. (4)

7 She works for a … of lawyers. (4)

10 What does he do … a living? (3)

12 Short for 'Confederation of British Industry' (3)

13 Unfortunately, it's a job with … prospects. (2)

14 He's lost his job. He got the … . (4)

15 He's lost his job. He's been made … . (9)

16 The things you have to do in a job. (6)

18 My grandfather worked in the steel … . (8)

Down ▼

2 The job was … in several newspapers. (10)

3 I'd like to … for the job. (5)

4 Who's your … manager? (4)

7 A workplace where things are made. (7)

8 What are the prospects for … in this company? (9)

9 I'm looking for a job. Do you have any … ? (9)

11 They've gone … strike. (2)

17 'Dear … / Madam' (3)

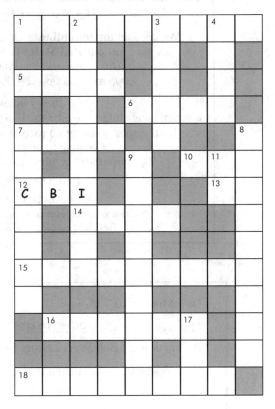

a working lunch

3

4a Read the advertisement and complete Cheryl's letter using the words in the box.

The Nottingham Gazette

Party assistants

We are looking for enthusiastic party assistants to work at our Bell Street Leisure Centre.

Hours of work: Saturday afternoons:
1.00p.m. to 3.00p.m., 4.00p.m. to 6.00p.m.

Duties include
● supervising children aged 3 to 10 ● organizing entertainment and team games ● setting up party decorations and equipment ● helping to prepare party food

Opportunities for: promotion to party supervisor

References required.

Applications in writing to:
Sandra Clarke, The Bell Street Leisure Centre,
Bell Street, Nottingham, NG2 7RP

enjoy
interested
hearing
keen
referees
relevant
spent
apply
studying
advertisement

Dear Mrs Clarke

I have just seen your [1] *advertisement* .... in the Nottingham Gazette for party assistants at the Bell Street Leisure Centre, and I would like to [2] ....

I am sixteen years old. I am a student at the County High School, where I am [3] .... for GCSEs in nine subjects.

I [4] .... working and playing with young children. I have [5] .... quite a lot of time during the school holidays looking after my cousins, who are six and four. Two of my GCSEs are in Art and Physical Education, which I imagine would be [6] .... to this job. I am very [7] .... on sports, especially team sports like basketball and football. I would be particularly [8] .... in becoming a party supervisor.

My PE teacher and a friend of my family's have agreed to act as [9] ....

I look forward to [10] .... from you.

Yours sincerely

C.Ramura

Cheryl Ramura

4b Write your own letter of application either for the job in 4a or for this job.

> ### Assistants required
>
> The Young Learners Centre is a study centre for children aged between 4 and 10. We are looking for assistants to mark the children's work in a variety of subjects, especially in Maths and Science.
>
> Please apply in writing, giving details of your experience, qualifications and interests and the names of two referees to Peter Duckworth, The Young Learners Centre, High Street, Barnet, HA8 9TR.

5a Use the words in the box to complete the text.

boss	colleagues	commission	company
prospects	strike	trade union	well-paid
head office	meetings	industrial estate	union representative

Hello! My name's May Cheung. I work as a travel agent for Pathfinders. It's a
¹ *company* .... which specializes in travel for young people. It's based in
Sanderstead, which is a very pleasant place. The ² .... is in
Croydon, in the middle of an ³ .... I'm glad I don't work there!

I like it here. It's a good job and it's ⁴ ....
My ⁵ .... are all quite young, so we socialize after work.
My ⁶ .... is nice, too. She'll always take time to explain things,
especially at the team ⁷ .... which we have every Monday morning.

We get a basic salary, but we can also earn ⁸ ...., depending on how many customers
we get. And the ⁹ .... for promotion are quite good.

I'm a member of a ¹⁰ .... In fact, I'm the ¹¹ .... Fortunately, we
don't have many problems here. We've never had to go on ¹² ....

5b Imagine yourself in a full-time job. Give an account of your working life, similar to May's.

6 Write ten words and five expressions you are going to memorize.

Words	Expressions
1	1 ....
2	....
3	2 ....
4	....
5	3 ....
6	....
7	4 ....
8	....
9	5 ....
10	....

4 Travelling and working abroad

Translate the words and phrases.

Travelling (verb phrases)

take a year out / a gap year

....

go on a working holiday

....

go on an expedition

....

go trekking

....

go backpacking

....

A gap year is a year between school and university.

Travel arrangements

passport ....

ticket ....

visa ....

work permit ....

itinerary ....

insurance (U) ....

accommodation (U) ....

U = a noun which is uncountable in this context.

REF *See also Boost Your Vocabulary 2, pages 64 – 65 (Holidays).*

Finding the money

I raised money by working as a waitress.

....

I spent several months doing odd jobs.

....

I got a temporary job.

....

I asked people to sponsor me.

....

I got sponsorship from several local companies.

....

I borrowed the money from ...

....

I got a loan from ...

....

Youth schemes

participant ....

assessment ....

responsibilities ....

selection criteria (*plural*) ....

voluntary work (U) ....

work experience (U) ....

I got in touch with (*name of an organization*).

....

I've been accepted to do voluntary work in (*country*).

....

I'm going on | a training course.
             | an orientation weekend.

....

Projects

archaeological work (U) ....   collecting scientific data ....

conservation work (U) ....   teaching ....

community work (U) ....   an adventure project ....

construction work (U) ....   an environmental project ....

Activities

mountaineering ....

bungee jumping ....

white-water rafting ....

scuba diving ....

Personal qualities

You need to be ... .

  adaptable ....

  enthusiastic ....

  curious ....

  self-motivated ....

  self-aware ....

  resilient ....

  realistic ....

  committed ....

  a team player ....

You need to have good communication skills.

....

Advantages of working abroad

I had an opportunity to see the world.

....

I met people from other cultures.

....

I became more independent.

....

I felt very grown-up.

....

I'm now much better at standing up for myself.

....

I learned a new skill. (e.g. carpentry)

....

It gave me | a sense of direction.
           | more confidence.

....

....

Questions to ask about projects

Is the work paid or is it voluntary?

....

What will my responsibilities be?

....

Who will benefit from this project?

....

What training will I receive?

....

Who is responsible for travel arrangements?

....

What about inoculations and health precautions?

....

....

Do I have to pay a deposit?

....

If I have a problem with my placement, who do I talk to?

....

....

What if there is an emergency?

....

How long has the organization existed?

....

Wayne's year out really gave him a sense of direction.

REF *See page 86 for the British / American word list.*

4

1 What are they?

1 It might be a house, or it might be a tent, but you'll need somewhere to stay! _accommodation_...............

2 You may need this as well as your passport to visit certain countries. ....

3 You will need this in case you are ill or lose your luggage. ....

4 You may need this document to allow you to get a job. ....

5 Your travel agent will give you this detailed list of flights and destinations. ....

6 You're working to help a particular group of people in a particular place. ....

7 You don't get paid for doing this type of work. ....

2a Read the extract from the leaflet and complete the words.

VOLUNTEERS FOR A BETTER WORLD

We're looking for people who are

☐ enth. _usiastic_......

☐ commi...................

☐ curi...................

☐ real...................

☐ res...................

☐ ada...................

☐ self-a...................

☐ self-mo...................

and above all, people who are

☐ t............... pl...............

and who have

☐ good co........................... skills

Which of these qualities do you have? Tick the boxes.

2b Choose the word or phrase from 2a which best describes these people.

1 I've never built a wall before, but I'll have a go. _adaptable_...............

2 That's a great idea! Let's do it! ....

3 I wonder what life in a village in the rainforest is like. ....

4 If I'm not feeling very well or if I've had a bad day, I don't let it bother me. I soon bounce back! ....

5 I'm quite good at starting new projects without much help from other people. ....

6 If I say I'll do something, I'll do it. ....

7 If I feel something is too difficult for me, I say so. ....

8 We like working as part of a group. ....

9 I know what my strengths and weaknesses are. ....

10 I find it easy to express myself. I've got ....

3 How did these people raise money for their year abroad? Use a different expression each time.

1 ....
....
working as a
waitress.

2 ....
....
....
....

3 ....
....
....
....

4 ....
....
....
....

5 ....
....
....
....
....

6 ....
....
....
....

> OK, you can pay me back when you get a job.

Which way would you choose to raise money? Rank them from A to F in order of preference (A = the best).

1 ☐   2 ☐   3 ☐   4 ☐   5 ☐   6 ☐

4a What type of work / holiday is described in these publicity extracts?

Do you want to help preserve the coral reef in Belize? You'll be part of a great team.

conservation work ....

Do you want to go trekking in the rainforest? Do you want to climb the magnificent Mount Kinabul? And then go white-water rafting and diving? Then Borneo is the place for you.

....

They want to learn your language, and you can learn theirs.
What are you waiting for?

....

Help us to count the number of black and white rhino left in Namibia. Come and take part in this major wildlife survey.

....

4b Write a similar short piece of publicity to encourage people to do archaeological work in Egypt.

5a What are Tom's plans? Write about them.

May	Exams, exams, exams
June	Training course to work for Sunsail
Jul – Aug	Summer job: sailing instructor. Money!
Sep – Nov	Odd jobs to earn more money
December	New Zealand! Backpacking, bungee jumping, white-water rafting, scuba diving … going from South Island to North Island.

In May he's going to take his exams. In June …

 5b Make a similar plan for yourself or someone you know. Be as ambitious as you like!

6 Read the extract from this website and answer the questions.

Expeditions for change

We have been organizing expeditions since 1980. Many of the volunteers have little or no experience of trekking, building or endangered species conservation. But they all share curiosity, enthusiasm and a willingness to learn.

If you are between 17 and 25 and able to raise the money to go, then you qualify to go on an expedition. It could be the chance of a lifetime for you. No special qualifications are required, but there will be a week's orientation course before you leave to assess your strengths and teach you basic skills.

Over a three-month period, volunteers will work on high-quality community and environmental projects. In each scheme there are fifteen volunteers and two project leaders.

Food and accommodation are provided, but you are not paid for the work you do. There will be two to four people in a room in one of our wooden huts.

Our insurance policy covers you for medical expenses, loss of baggage and personal possessions. A copy of the policy can be sent to you. If necessary, we will arrange for you to return home as soon as possible.

Six months before you go, you need to pay ten per cent of the cost of the trip.

1 How many people are there in each scheme?
Fifteen volunteers and two project leaders.
....

2 Do you have to have relevant experience to apply for a place?
....

3 What sort of personal qualities are needed?
....

4 How long are you away for?
....

5 What sort of work is involved?
....

6 What training will you receive?
....

7 What is the accommodation like?
....

8 What if there is an emergency – if you're ill, for example?
....

9 How can you check the details of the insurance policy?
....

10 Do you have to pay a deposit in advance? If so, how much?
....

7 What would your ideal three-month expedition be? Answer the questions.

- Where would you go?
- What would you do?
- How would you raise the money?
- What would the advantages of such an expedition be for you?

8 Write ten words and five expressions you are going to memorize.

Words	Expressions
1	1 ....
2	....
3	2 ....
4	....
5	3 ....
6	....
7	4 ....
8	....
9	5 ....
10	....

Test yourself 1 (Units 1 to 4)

How much can you remember?

My mark: _____
60

1 What are they? Describe each item without using the word *piece(s)*.

0   a *segment*.. of orange   6   some .... of rice

1   a .... of beef   7   a .... of lemon juice

2   a .... of bread   8   sugar ....

3   a .... of butter   9   a .... of grapes

4   a .... of chocolate   10   bread..........

5   a .... of salt

(10 marks)

2 Complete the sentences with the correct prepositions.

in	on	for	with	up	up	in	on	for	with	up

0   You always stand *up*.......... for your best friend.

1   Are you going .... holiday this summer?

2   Did you get .... touch with your American cousin?

3   Do you get on well .... your older sister?

4   He and his girlfriend split .... last year.

5   He fell .... love with a girl he met on holiday.

6   I'm going .... a training course next weekend.

7   There's something wrong .... the CD player.

8   They were brought .... by their grandmother.

9   What do you do .... a living?

10   When are you available .... interview?

(10 marks)

3 Complete the words to describe these people.

0   'I've had some disappointments, but I always manage to keep going.'   r e _s i l i e n t_

1   'Just do as I say.'   b o _ _ _

2   'I just can't walk into a room full of strangers.'   s _ _

3   'I hate it when you look at other boys. You're mine.'   p o _ _ _ _ _ _ _

4   'I always play to win.'   c o _ _ _ _ _ _ _ _

5   'I'm quite happy travelling on my own.'   i n _ _ _ _ _ _ _ _ _

6 'I'm always interested in finding out more.'   c u _ _ _ _ _

7 'I think I know myself quite well.'   s _ _ _-a w _ _ _

8 'Don't talk to me about kindness.
    People only do things for selfish reasons.'   c y _ _ _ _ _

9 'I have to say what I think.'   f r _ _ _

10 'Great! Fantastic! Let's go now!'   e n _ _ _ _ _ _ _ _ _

(10 marks)

---

4 **Name one thing which**

0	crackles	*wood on a fire*
1	ticks	....
2	rings	....
3	buzzes	....
4	hisses	....

Name two things which can get

8	flooded	...................., ...
9	torn	...................., ...
10	blocked	...................., ...
11	dented	...................., ...

(15 marks)

Name one thing which can

5	shrink	....
6	leak	....
7	go wrong	....

5 **Complete the conversation.**

Mum: There's an ⁰ *advert* .... in the newspaper for jobs at Compushop. They say they've got two ¹.................... for sales assistants. Why don't you ²....................?

Sara: But I haven't done anything like that before. I haven't got any 'relevant ³....................'.

Mum: I'm sure there'll be a training ⁴.................... . Go on, send off for an ⁵.................... form and a job ⁶...................., to see what you have to do.

Sara: But I'll need two ⁷.................... – you know, people who will write nice things about me!

Mum: Well, you can ask your English teacher and Susanne's dad. After all, he's the managing ⁸.................... of a big company.

Sara: Yes, I know.

Mum: Look, you want to save some money for your gap year, don't you? And you don't want to spend months just doing odd ⁹.................... and earning very little.

Sara: I thought I could get a ¹⁰.................... from the bank.

Mum: And have you thought about paying it back? Anyway, it's not good to ¹¹.................... money if you don't have to.

Sara: Well, perhaps I could get ¹².................... from companies like the one dad works for.

Mum: Maybe you could. But this will mean you've got some extra money for all the things you want to do.

Sara: Like scuba ¹³.................... and white-water ¹⁴...................., you mean?

Mum: Exactly.

Sara: Well, I suppose it's better than working as a ¹⁵.................... in a restaurant.

(15 marks)

5 Looking after the body

Translate the words and phrases.

Keeping fit and healthy

do regular exercise ....

work out (at the gym) ....

warm up ....

stretch ....

cool down ....

eat healthily ....

avoid stress ....

relax ....

I don't mind warming up and cooling down. It's the bit in between that I don't like.

A healthy diet

vitamins ....

minerals ....

carbohydrates ....

fats ....

proteins ....

fibre ....

The body

bones ....

joints ....

muscles ....

Internal organs

brain ....

lungs ....

heart ....

liver ....

kidneys ....

stomach ....

Circulation of the blood

blood ....

vein ....

artery ....

pulse ....

high / low blood pressure

....

Hygiene

wash your hair ....

cut your nails ....

file your nails ....

have a shower ....

have a wash ....

shave ....

clean / brush your teeth ....

Hygiene products

cotton wool ....

deodorant ....

cleanser ....

soap ....

shower gel ....

shampoo ....

conditioner ....

toothpaste ....

toothbrush ....

razor ....

shaving cream ....

nail file ....

nail scissors ....

nail clippers ....

washbag ....

Physical sensations and states

Noun phrases

sharp / acute pain ....

dull ache ....

irritation ....

stiffness ....

tenderness ....

Verb phrases

ache ....

shake ....

shiver ....

sweat ....

throb ....

be / feel ...

   well ....

   poorly ....

   under the weather ....

be ...

   fit and healthy ....

   in good health ....

   in poor health ....

have (got) a fever

....

Some serious illnesses and diseases

have (got) ... .

   asthma ....

   diabetes ....

   arthritis ....

   cancer ....

   heart disease ....

   hepatitis ....

   malaria ....

   cholera ....

   typhoid ....

   AIDS ....

He had a heart attack.

....

He had a stroke.

....

He's HIV+ (positive).

....

REF *See also* **Boost Your Vocabulary 3**, *pages 24 – 25 (Health).*

Illness *is a general term which covers conditions like asthma;* **diseases** *affect particular parts of the body (e.g. heart disease) or can be caught (e.g. typhoid).*

Treatment

conventional medicine

....

alternative medicine / complementary medicine

....

go into hospital

....

have an operation (on)

....

take medicine / tablets

....

take a course of antibiotics

....

have physiotherapy ....

recover ....

feel better ....

get better ....

get over an illness ....

REF *See page 86 for the British / American word list.*

HYGIENE ROUTINE

HYGIENE ROUTINE...HYGIENE ROUTINE...HYGIENE ROUTIN...

How often do you...?

1a Write about your hygiene routine.

Products used

① *I wash my hair twice a week.* .... *shampoo, conditioner* ....

② ....

③ ....

④ ....

⑤ ....

⑥ ....

⑦ ....

Which other hygiene products do you use on a regular basis?

....

1b How do you keep fit and healthy? Think of
    a your diet   **b** your daily routine   **c** the exercise you do.

b I avoid stress.   *I get my dad to do my homework.*

Activity   **Example**

....

....

....

....

....

2a Label the diagram.

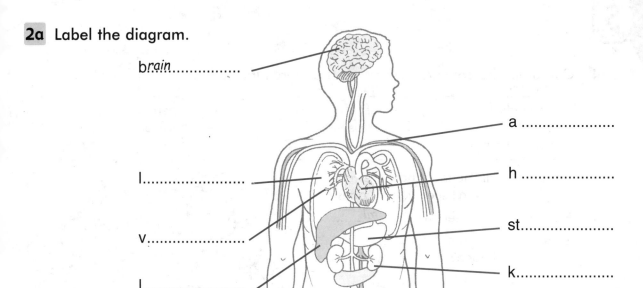

brain................

a ....

h ....

l.....................

st.....................

v.....................

k.....................

l.....................

2b Use the words from 2a to complete the chart.

Part of the body	Function
1 ...the liver......	It weighs about two kilos and it is where food is stored or processed.
2	They carry blood from the heart to the rest of the body.
3	It is like a bag in which food is changed into liquid.
4	They filter the blood and get rid of waste liquid.
5	They carry blood to the heart from the rest of the body.
6	It pumps the blood around the body.
7	You have two, and you need them to breathe.
8	It controls everything you do.

3 What does each group of foods provide?

proteins   **fat**   **minerals**   **fibre**   **vitamin C**   **carbohydrates**

nuts   fish
...*minerals*...
cereals   salt

apples   lemons
....
tomatoes   oranges

cheese   yoghurt
....
butter   cream

pasta   bread
....
potatoes   rice

fish   eggs
....
meat   soya

bread   fruit
....
cereal   vegetables

4 Complete the conversation using the words in the box.

appendicitis	fit	operation
better	hospital	recovered
conventional	life	serious

Simon: Hi, Hannah, how are you? I haven't seen you for ages.

Hannah: I've been in ¹. *hospital* .

Simon: Oh, nothing ²......................., I hope?

Hannah: I had ³..........................

Simon: Did you have an ⁴..........................?

Hannah: Yes, I did.

Simon: But I thought you didn't believe in ⁵..........................medicine.

Hannah: Well, when it's a matter of ⁶.......................... or death, you sometimes don't have a choice!

Simon: Yes, I see. Have you ⁷..........................?

Hannah: Yes, I feel much ⁸.........................., thanks.

Simon: Did I ever tell you about my operation? I've still got the scar. Look!

Hannah: Sorry, Simon, I must go. Bye.

5 Complete the words and expressions.

1 'He's under the weather' means *He doesn't feel very well* .

2 ..*'She's sh*..........................' means 'She's shaking because she's so cold'.

3 You can see that he's got a fever because *he's sw*..........................

4 You don't say a 'strong' pain; you say *a*.......................... *pain* .

5 You don't say a 'soft' ache; you say *a*.......................... *ache* .

6 What should you do before exercise? .... *up* .

7 What should you do after exercise? .... *down* .

8 Stay away from stressful situations; in other words, ... *stress* .

9 If your skin itches, you have a skin .*i*..........................

10 Footballers often have physiotherapy to treat *st*.......................... in their joints.

6 Try this quiz.

So you want to be a doctor? ✚

① Name a disease that affects the stomach and is caused by bad water.
cholera ....

② Name an illness that causes difficulties in breathing. ....

③ Name a disease which can be caused by smoking. ....

④ This disease causes a lot of pain in the joints of your bones. ....

⑤ Which disease is associated with some types of mosquito? ....

⑥ Which disease affects your liver, causes fever and makes your skin look yellow? ....

⑦ If you have too much sugar in your blood, what are you suffering from? ....

⑧ If you have high blood pressure, what are the dangers if it is not treated? ....

Which is true? Tick the correct option.

① Antibiotics are effective in treating ☐ viruses. ☐ bacterial infections.

② The body ☐ can ☐ can't store vitamin C.

③ HIV is a kind of virus that can cause ☐ AIDS. ☐ hepatitis.

④ If you are overweight, you may develop ☐ high blood pressure. ☐ low blood pressure.

Check your answers on page D.

7 Write ten words and five expressions you are going to memorize.

Words	Expressions
1	1 ....
2	....
3	2 ....
4	....
5	3 ....
6	....
7	4 ....
8	....
9	5 ....
10	....

6 Society

Translate the words and phrases.

Social events

(family) gathering	....
get-together	....
party	....
celebration	....
reunion	....
anniversary	....
wedding	....
funeral	....

Special interest groups

I've joined / I'm a member of / I belong to / I'm in a (an) ...

(football) team

....

(chess) club

....

(local history) society

....

(political) party

....

(international) organization

....

(environmental) group

....

Generations

generation gap	....
the older / younger generation	....
age group	....
peer group	....

Social classes (in Britain)

the aristocracy	....
the upper class	....
the middle class	....
the working class	....

from a (working-class) background

....

from an aristocratic background

....

the rich	....
the poor	....

the (general) public ....

Perhaps I'm descended from the aristocracy!

INTERNET CAFÉ

FAMILY HISTORY WEBSITE

Yes, we've all heard of Queen Tracy the First.

Civilization

the human race ....
population ....
community ....
culture ....
people ....

> *People* can be used to mean people **generally**, e.g. *How many people were at the concert?* and to refer to those belonging to a **particular** nation or race, e.g. *The people of Britain demand a referendum. Both take plural verbs.*

Concepts

society ....
individual ....
identity ....
rights ....
responsibilities ....
the right to vote ....
liberty ....
freedom of speech ....
censorship ....
justice ....
equality ....
law and order ....
wealth ....
poverty ....

> An *identity card* is sometimes called an **ID card**. The opposites of *justice* and *equality* are *injustice* and *inequality*.

The spirit of the age

liberal ....
progressive ....
conservative ....
repressive ....
permissive ....
tolerant ....
revolutionary ....

International / internal relations

war ....
peace ....
revolution ....
globalization ....

Bad behaviour

> When people refer to **a youth** or a **gang of youths**, they are talking about young men whose behaviour they disapprove of. But **youth** can be used to talk about young people generally, without implying an attitude on the part of the speaker, e.g. **youth culture, the youth of the country, in his youth** ... .

youth ....
bully ....
lout ....
thug ....
(football) hooligan ....
vandal ....
be in a gang ....

 REF See also Unit 8, The law and crime, page 50.

Social issues

crime ....
prejudice ....
racism ....
sexism ....
vandalism ....
drug addiction ....
drunkenness ....
homelessness ....
violence ....

 REF See page 86 for the British / American word list.

1a What sort of social event are these people at?

1

> It's lovely to have you all here –
> brothers, sisters, uncles, aunts, cousins.

<u>a family gathering / a family get-together</u>

2

> Happy birthday to you!

....

3

> We were in the same class at primary
> school, and it's ten years since we've
> seen each other.

....

4

> You are now husband and wife.

....

5

> Here's to another 25 years of
> happily married life!

....

6

> It's a sad day, but at least she's at
> peace now.

....

1b Complete the sentences using the words in the box.

organization	gang	club	party	society	team

1 I go to photography *club*..................... after school on Wednesdays.

2 No, I don't belong to a political ....

3 There was a .... of about ten youths in leather jackets hanging around.

4 I belong to the debating .... at school.

5 Which football .... do you support?

6 Amnesty International is an .... which defends human rights.

2a Write in the correct class description.

The 1950s in Britain

Case studies	Which class did they belong to?
1 Penelope Montcrieff went to a private school. She has never worked, but she owns a large country house which is open to the public.	*the upper class* ....
2 Ron Jenkins is a car mechanic. He rents a flat in a London suburb.	....
3 Henry and June Baker met at university. Henry is a bank manager and June is a housewife.	....
4 Lady Fortescue is related to the Royal Family.	....

2b Read what these people say. Then write about social classes in your country today.

We live in a classless society. There are the rich and the poor, and most of us are in between.

Britain today is just one big middle class. But it's hard for people from immigrant families to be accepted into it.

Of course there are still social classes in Britain. If you work with your hands, you're working class; if you work in an office, you're middle class; and if you don't work, you're upper class.

3a Complete the text using the words in the box.

background	drunkenness	gap	poor	population
poverty	responsibilities	rich	right	wealth

1900 - 1914

At the turn of the twentieth century, about a quarter of the [1] *population* of Britain was living in [2] .... For those people, life was hard. Some of them turned to alcohol. Saturday nights in the towns were often disturbed by [3] .... and rioting. The [4] .... between the [5] .... and the [6] .... was enormous.

Only men with some [7] .... could vote. Women did not have the [8] .... to vote until 1918 (and even then they had to be over 30); yet in 1900 there were over 200 women doctors and over 100 women dentists. They were therefore given [9] .... but could not choose or be part of the government of the country.

People from a working class [10] .... were expected to touch their caps if they met one of their social superiors.

3b Write about similar social changes in your country in the last century. Try to use some of the words from the box in 3a.

....

....

....

6

4 Read Jade's answers to this questionnaire. Then give your own answers.

Questionnaire
Society today – let's hear your views.

1 Would you describe your country as
a) liberal?   b) forward-looking?   c) conservative?   d) *other*

> *Conservative - even though we have a Labour government.*

2 Would you describe your society as
a) repressive?   b) permissive?   c) tolerant?   d) *other*

> *Fairly tolerant, but also quite violent.*

3 Which are the biggest problems in your society? Number them from 1 to 6
(1 = most serious)

③ ☐ racism	① ☐ drug addiction	⑥ ☐ vandalism
⑤ ☐ sexism	② ☐ violence	④ ☐ homelessness

4 Compare your generation with your grandparents'.
a) Community spirit – stronger now or then?

> *Among young people, stronger now.*

b) Easier to be an individual – now or then?

> *Much easier now.*

c) Freedom of speech – more now or then?

> *More now.*

d) Law and order – better now or then?

> *No difference. It's just that crimes are reported more in our newspapers and on TV.*

e) Generation gap between parents and children – greater now or then?

> *Probably greater then. But I get on better with my grandparents than with my parents sometimes!*

5 Solve the crossword.

Across ▶

1   If you are very poor, you live in ... .
    (7)

4   What was life like ... the 1960s? (2)

5   Friends of the Earth is ...
    environmental organization. (2)

6   She's Japanese and he's English.
    Their ... are different, but they get on
    very well. (8)

7   It can mean *the time when you are
    young*; it can also refer to a young
    man who behaves badly. (5)

8   We're all part of the human race.
    You shouldn't think of *them and
    ...* . (2)

11 Are you employed part-time or ...-
    time? (4)

12 Don't give in to peer-... pressure. (5)

14 Do you belong ... a political party?
    (2)

15 When there is no prejudice, you have
    ... . (8)

16 ... *card* is short for *identity card*. (2)

17 What does the ... public think of the
    government's plans? (7)

¹P	²O	V	E	R	T	³y		⁴	
⁵		⁶							
⁷							⁸		
					⁹				
¹⁰				¹¹					
¹²			¹³						
						¹⁴			
	¹⁵								
¹⁶		¹⁷							

Down ▼

1   A political group, and a celebration. (5)

2   I'm doing a project ... the environment. (2)

3   You need to know ... rights and
    responsibilities. (4)

4   The opposite of *15 Across*. (10)

6   An organization for people who share an
    interest. (4)

9   Fairness in the law. (7)

10 Are you in the 18 to 30 ... group? Then this
    holiday is for you! (3)

13 The opposite of *war*. (5)

15 Well done! You've reached the ... ! (3)

6 Write ten words and five expressions you are going to memorize.

Words	Expressions
1	1 ....
2	....
3	2 ....
4	....
5	3 ....
6	....
7	4 ....
8	....
9	5 ....
10	....

People and politics

Translate the words and phrases.

Politics and geography

country ....

state ....

empire ....

nation ....

border ....

... we'd be living in a police state.

If I were the Prime Minister ...

Systems of government

monarchy ....

republic ....

democracy ....

dictatorship ....

police state ....

military rule ....

the (Bush)
  administration ....

Political philosophies

socialism / socialist ....

capitalism / capitalist ....

communism / communist ....

Political groups and organizations

political party ....

the government ....

the opposition ....

a coalition government ....

People in politics

politician ....

Democrat
(*adj*: democratic) ....

Republican
(*adj*: republican) ....

President ....

Vice-President ....

Prime Minister ....

Deputy Prime Minister ....

Member of Parliament
(MP) ....

monarch ....

emperor ....

dictator ....

government minister ....

leader (of a party /
country) ....

member of a party ....

Local government

mayor ....

councillor ....

Diplomatic and civil service

ambassador ....

diplomat ....

civil servant ....

> You can use a singular or plural verb after
> **government:**
> The government **has / have** failed to help the
> poorest in society.
> **Politics** is singular when it refers to a subject of
> study or a career. It is plural when it refers to
> someone's particular beliefs or a set of ideas.
> Politics **is** a popular subject at this university.
> Politics **is** my life.
> Let's just say that your politics **are** different from
> mine.
> The politics of the situation **are** quite complicated.

Answer key

1 People and relationships

Exercise 1
1 *considerate*
2 faithful
3 sociable
4 trustworthy
5 outgoing
6 frank
7 spiteful
9 two-faced
9 unsure
10 submissive

Exercise 2
Possible answers

good	bad	sometimes good, sometimes bad
affectionate self-confident faithful unselfconscious helpful	aggressive dependent unsociable inconsiderate	talkative romantic assertive reserved unromantic competitive

Exercise 3
1 *secretive*
2 malicious
3 meek
4 popular
5 independent
6 bossy
7 sympathetic
8 possessive
9 quiet
10 cold

Exercise 4a
1 *fell out with*
2 gets on with
3 's been going out with
4 split up with
5 look down on
6 'll stand up for
7 looks up to

Exercise 4b
a *2*; b 5; c 4; d 7

Exercise 5

Scoring: **1** a2, b1, c3 **2** a3, b2, c1 **3** a2, b1, c3 **4** a3, b1, c2 **5** a1, b3, c 2 **6** a3, b2, c1

Analysis:

Between 16 and 18	It's a surprise you've got time to do this questionnaire! You're popular, but are you independent enough?
Between 9 and 15	You relate to others well, and you have just the right amount of self-confidence.
Between 6 and 8	You're sympathetic and considerate. Are you perhaps a bit shy sometimes?

Exercise 6a
Person A: *fall in love*; be love at first sight; get engaged; get married; have
Person B: go out with; stay together; die; break up
Person C: don't believe; marry; get divorced; can't stand

Exercise 6b
Person A: romantic, sociable
Person B: faithful, trusting
Person C: cold, cynical

Exercise 7
1 *She was born in London in 1917.*
2 She was brought up by her grandparents.
3 She was educated at the local grammar school.
4 She went to college, but she still lived at home.
5 She left home when she was 18.
6 She started work at an engineering firm in 1938.
7 She got married in 1946 and had two children.
8 She retired in 1977.
9 She and her husband moved house in 1978.
10 She died in 2001.

2 Everyday life

Exercise 1a
1 b *a slice of cake*
2 d a bar of chocolate
3 e a bunch of grapes
4 c a squeeze of lemon juice
5 j a pinch of salt
6 f a joint of meat
7 a a lump of butter
8 i a grain of rice
9 h a segment of orange
10 g a drop of milk

Exercise 2a
1 *bar*
2 pane
3 sliver
4 sheet
5 scrap
6 speck
7 splinter
8 blade
9 blocks

Exercise 2b
1 *wisp*   2 pile   3 stack   4 heap   5 bundle

Exercise 3a
1 *is stuck.*
2 is burnt / burned.
3 is smashed / broken.
4 stain.
5 are ripped.
6 is damaged.
7 is dented.
8 is leaking.

Exercise 3b
1 *You'll have to call the engineer.*
2 Throw it away and start again.
3 You'll have to get it replaced.
4 Take it to the dry cleaner's.
5 You'll have to get them mended.
6 You'll have to take it back to the shop.
7 You'll have to get someone to look at it and tell you how much the repair will cost.
8 Buy a new one.

Exercise 4
flooded *a road*; a kitchen
torn a piece of paper; a bank note
blocked *a road*; a sink; a toilet
shrunk a jumper; a computer image

Exercise 5
1 *crack*
2 rustle
3 buzz
4 crackle
5 ring
6 splash
7 tick
8 fizz
9 pop
10 crash

Exercise 6a
1 *crunched*
2 jingled
3 snapped
4 hissed
5 whirr

3 The business world

Exercise 1a

managing director
finance director; sales director; marketing director
accounts manager; human resources manager;
production manager
sales representatives; technical support staff;
admin(istrative) staff

Exercise 1b

1 *the managing director*
2 the production manager
3 the finance director
4 the marketing director
5 the sales director
6 the accounts manager
7 sales representatives
8 the human resources manager
9 admin(istrative) staff
10 technical support staff

Exercise 2a

1 c *a freelance editor*
2 d a law firm
3 b a managing director
4 f a self-employed plumber
5 i admin staff
6 h a union representative
7 e a well-paid job
8 g to be made redundant
9 j to go on strike
10 a to work on commission

Exercise 3

¹A	V	²A	I	L	³A	B	⁴L	E
		D			P		I	
⁵H	A	V	E		P		N	
		E		⁶B	L	U	E	
⁷F	I	R	M		Y			⁸P
A		T		⁹V		¹⁰F	¹¹O	R
¹²C	B	I		A			¹³N	O
T		¹⁴S	A	C	K			M
O		E		A				O
¹⁵R	E	D	U	N	D	A	N	T
Y				C				I
	¹⁶D	U	T	I	E	¹⁷S		O
				E		I		N
¹⁸I	N	D	U	S	T	R	Y	

Exercise 4a

1 *advertisement*   6 relevant
2 apply   7 keen
3 studying   8 interested
4 enjoy   9 referees
5 spent   10 hearing

Exercise 5a

1 *company*   7 meetings
2 head office   8 commission
3 industrial estate   9 prospects
4 well-paid   10 trade union
5 colleagues   11 union representative
6 boss   12 strike

4 Travelling and working abroad

Exercise 1

1 *accommodation*   5 itinerary
2 visa   6 community work
3 insurance   7 voluntary work
4 work permit

Exercise 2a

enthusiastic, committed, curious, realistic, resilient,
adaptable, self-aware, self-motivated;
team players; good communication skills

Exercise 2b

1 *adaptable*   7 realistic
2 enthusiastic   8 team players
3 curious   9 self-aware
4 resilient   10 good communication skills
5 self-motivated
6 committed

Exercise 3
Possible answers

1 She raised money by *working as a waitress.*
2 He got a temporary job.
3 He spent several months doing odd jobs.
4 She got sponsorship from local companies. /
   She asked local companies to sponsor her.
5 He borrowed money.
6 She got a loan (from the bank).

Exercise 4a

Do you want to help preserve the coral reef in Belize? You'll be part of a great team. — *conservation work*

Do you want to go trekking in the rainforest? Do you want to climb the magnificent Mount Kinabul? And then go white-water rafting and diving? Then Borneo is the place for you. — adventure project

Help us to count the number of black and white rhino left in Namibia. Come and take part in this major wildlife survey. — environmental project

They want to learn your language, and you can learn theirs. **What are you waiting for?** — teaching

Exercise 5a
Possible answer

In May he's going to take his exams. In June he's doing a training course to work for Sunsail. Then in July and August, he's going to do a summer job as a sailing instructor. He's hoping to earn a lot of money! From September to November he's going to do some odd jobs to earn some more money and then, finally, in December he's going on holiday to New Zealand. He's going backpacking and he's hoping to do bungee jumping, white-water rafting, scuba diving, and lots more adventurous activities. He's going to travel all the way from South Island to North Island in New Zealand.

Exercise 6

1 *Fifteen volunteers and two project leaders.*
2 No. (But you have to be between 17 and 25 and able to raise the money to go.)
3 Curiosity, enthusiasm and a willingness to learn.
4 Three months.
5 High-quality community and environmental projects.
6 There will be a one-week orientation course before you leave.
7 You will share a room in a wooden hut with two to four people.
8 You will be covered (for medical expenses, loss of baggage and personal possessions) by an insurance policy.
9 You can ask for a copy of the policy to be sent to you.
10 Yes, you have to pay ten per cent of the cost of the trip six months before you go.

Test yourself 1 (Units 1 to 4)

Exercise 1

0	*segment*	6	grains
1	joint	7	squeeze
2	slice	8	lumps
3	lump	9	bunch
4	bar	10	crumbs
5	pinch		

Exercise 2

0	*up*	4	up	8	up
1	on	5	in	9	for
2	in	6	on	10	for
3	with	7	with		

Exercise 3

0	*resilient*	6	curious
1	bossy	7	self-aware
2	shy	8	cynical
3	possessive	9	frank
4	competitive	10	enthusiastic
5	independent		

Exercise 4

0	*wood on a fire*	6	a washing machine
1	a clock	7	a TV
2	a bell	8	a kitchen, a road
3	a bee	9	a shirt, a piece of paper
4	a snake	10	a sink, a toilet
5	a shirt	11	a car, a can (of soup)

Exercise 5

0	*advert*	8	director
1	vacancies	9	jobs
2	apply	10	loan
3	experience	11	borrow
4	course	12	sponsorship
5	application	13	diving
6	description	14	rafting
7	referees	15	waitress

5 Looking after the body

Exercise 1a
Possible answers

1 *I wash my hair twice a week; shampoo, conditioner*
2 I cut my nails (once a week); nail scissors / nail clippers
3 I file my nails (once a week); nail file
4 I brush my teeth (twice a day); toothbrush, toothpaste
5 I have a wash (every evening); cleanser, cotton wool, soap
6 I have a shower (every morning); shower gel, soap
7 I shave (every morning); razor, shaving cream

Exercise 2a

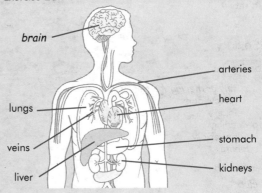

brain
arteries
heart
lungs
stomach
veins
kidneys
liver

Exercise 2b

1	*the liver*	4	the kidneys	7	lungs
2	arteries	5	veins	8	the brain
3	the stomach	6	the heart		

Exercise 3

nuts fish ....*minerals*.... cereals salt	apples lemons ....vitamin C.... tomatoes oranges
cheese yoghurt ....fat......... butter cream	pasta bread carbohydrates potatoes rice
fish eggs ....proteins.... meat soya	bread fruit ....fibre.... cereal vegetables

Exercise 4

1 *hospital*
2 serious
3 appendicitis
4 operation
5 conventional
6 life
7 recovered
8 better

Exercise 5

1 'He doesn't feel very well.'
2 'She's sh*ivering*'
3 he's sw*eating*
4 a sharp *pain*
5 a dull *ache*
6 warm *up*
7 cool *down*
8 avoid *stress*
9 *irr*itation
10 *st*iffness

Exercise 6

1 *cholera*
2 asthma
3 (lung) cancer
4 arthritis
5 malaria
6 hepatitis
7 diabetes
8 a heart attack
    a stroke

1 bacterial infections
2 can't
3 AIDS
4 high blood pressure

6 Society

Exercise 1a

1 *a family gathering / a family get-together*
2 a (birthday) party
3 a reunion
4 a wedding
5 an anniversary
6 a funeral

Exercise 1b

1 *club*
2 party
3 gang
4 society
5 team
6 organization

Exercise 2a

1 *the upper class*
2 the working class
3 the middle class
4 the aristocracy

Exercise 3a

1 *population*
2 poverty
3 drunkenness
4 gap
5 rich
6 poor
7 wealth
8 right
9 responsibilities
10 background

Exercise 5

1P	2O	V	E	R	T	Y		3Y		4I	N
5A	N							O		N	
R		6C	U	L	T	U	R	E	S		
T		L				R		Q			
7Y	O	U	T	H					8U	S	
		B				9J		A			
10A				11F	U	L	L				
12G	R	O	U	13P		S		I			
E				E		T		14T	O		
	15E	Q	U	A	L	I	T	Y			
	N			C		C					
16I	D		17G	E	N	E	R	A	L		

7 People and politics

Exercise 1

1 c *Prime Minister*
2 e Vice President
3 d opinion poll
4 f proportional representation
5 g civil servant
6 b campaign slogan
7 a general election
8 h government minister

Exercise 2

1 emperor
2 monarch
3 dictatorship
4 Prime Minister
5 Prime Minister
6 President, Republican

Exercise 3

1 *mayor*
2 ambassador
3 diplomat
4 civil servant
5 candidate
6 floating voter
7 demonstrator
8 campaigner
9 opinion poll
10 election
11 referendum
12 coalition
13 communist
14 capitalist
15 socialist

L	U	D	R	E	P	C	O	A	L	I	T	I	O	N
E	F	L	O	A	T	I	N	G	V	O	T	E	R	U
C	A	M	P	A	I	G	N	E	R	T	M	Y	O	R
A	P	C	I	V	I	L	S	E	R	V	A	N	T	E
N	M	S	N	T	O	M	O	L	J	C	M	T	L	F
D	R	W	I	P	B	U	C	E	P	W	B	V	C	E
I	R	P	O	L	I	T	I	C	S	M	A	Y	O	R
D	E	H	N	R	S	P	A	T	D	O	S	L	M	E
A	C	A	P	I	T	A	L	I	S	T	S	O	M	N
T	A	R	O	L	H	U	I	O	P	J	A	P	U	D
E	E	P	L	R	Y	L	S	N	Y	E	D	I	N	U
D	I	P	L	O	M	A	T	T	N	C	O	X	I	M
D	E	M	O	N	S	T	R	A	T	O	R	R	L	S
I	T	U	E	W	E	N	A	K	P	S	W	R	T	L

Exercise 4a

1. *extreme left*
2. left of centre
3. centre
4. right of centre
5. extreme right
6. left wing
7. right wing

Exercise 5

1. *stood*
2. election
3. candidates
4. campaign
5. slogan
6. held
7. neck
8. neck
9. vote
10. wing
11. party
12. seat

8 The law and crime

Exercise 1a

1. *a magistrate*
2. a solicitor
3. a barrister
4. a police officer
5. a detective

Exercise 1b

1. *the chairman of the jury*
2. the judge
3. a witness
4. the defendant
5. the defence
6. the prosecution

Exercise 2

1. *He went to the pub with his friends on his eighteenth birthday.*
2. He drove home.
3. He was stopped by the police.
4. They arrested him.
5. He was charged with drink driving.
6. He appeared in court.
7. He pleaded guilty.
8. He was fined and banned from driving for two years.

Exercise 3

	¹A	G	²A	I	N	³S	T
⁴O	N		N			E	
	D			⁵M		⁶N	O
⁷I		⁸C	O	U	R	T	
N		U		R		E	
N		⁹R	I	D	I	N	G
O		F		E		C	
¹⁰C	L	E	A	R		E	
E		W				¹¹D	¹²O
N			¹³I	N			F
¹⁴T	H	E	F	T		¹⁵O	F

Exercise 4

1	*13*	6	14	11	16	16	16
2	16	7	18	12	17	17	16
3	10	8	12	13	18	18	16
4	15	9	16	14	17	19	18
5	18	10	18	15	16	20	18

Test yourself 2 (Units 5 to 8)

Exercise 1

0. *some shower gel*
1. soap
2. shampoo (and) conditioner
3. toothbrush (and) toothpaste
4. razor (and) shaving cream
5. scissors / nail clippers

Exercise 2

Internal organs	Illnesses and diseases	Physical sensations and states
0 *brain*		
1 heart	6 asthma	11 ache
2 kidneys	7 cholera	12 irritation
3 liver	8 diabetes	13 pain
4 lungs	9 hepatitis	14 stiffness
5 stomach	10 typhoid	15 tenderness

Exercise 3

Possible answers

1. a (family) gathering, a party, a celebration, a reunion, an anniversary, a wedding, a funeral
2. a football team, a chess club, a local history society, a political party, an international organization, an environmental group
3. crime, prejudice, racism, sexism, vandalism, drunkenness, homelessness, violence
4. republic, democracy, dictatorship, police state, military rule
5. the middle class, the working class, the aristocracy

Exercise 4

0. *right*
1. identity / ID
2. freedom
3. law
4. power
5. opposition
6. poll
7. gap

Exercise 5

0. *a fraudster*
1. a burglar
2. a murderer
3. a thief
4. a police officer
5. a detective
6. a witness
7. a victim
8. the chairman of the jury
9. the judge
10. the defence

Exercise 6

0. *into*
1. taken
2. charged
3. innocent
4. evidence
5. trial
6. court
7. pleaded
8. jury
9. verdict
10. sentenced

9 Newspapers and magazines

Exercise 1a

	Articles	Visuals
1 jou_rnal_is_t	✓	–
2 photog_r a p h e r_	–	✓
3 re_por_ter	✓	–
4 d_esig_ner	–	✓
5 r_e_v_ie_wer	✓	–
6 i_l l_u_s t r a_tor	–	✓
7 car_too_ni_s t	–	✓
8 co_r r e s p o_ndent	✓	–

Exercise 2a
Possible answers (in Britain)

1 The Times
2 The Evening Standard (for London)
3 Vogue
4 Smash Hits
5 Private Eye
6 Time Out
7 What Car?
8 Suga Babes
9 New Scientist
10 The Beano

Exercise 4a

 balanced
entertaining
fair

 biased
intrusive
sensationalist

Exercise 4b

1 intrusive
2 sensationalist
3 fair
4 entertaining

Exercise 5a

1a *the financial section*
1b *the economics editor*
2a world news
2b the foreign correspondent
3a the travel section
3b the travel correspondent
4a home news
4b the crime correspondent
5a the fashion section
5b the fashion editor
6a the sports section
6b the sports reporter
7a features
7b the consumer affairs editor

Exercise 6

1 *a weather forecast*
2 the horoscopes
3 a film review
4 a competition
5 an editorial
6 an obituary

Exercise 7
Possible answers

1 Rich banks rob the poor
2 the TMX trekker

10 Books

Exercise 1a

1 *a contemporary novel*
2 an atlas
3 a short story
4 a ghost story
5 a biography
6 a thriller
7 a travel book
8 a historical novel
9 a guidebook
10 a cookbook
11 a reference book
12 a dictionary
13 a romantic novel
14 a detective story
15 an encyclopedia
16 science fiction

Exercise 1b

Fiction	Non-fiction
a contemporary novel	an atlas
a short story	a biography
a ghost story	a travel book
a thriller	a guidebook
a historical novel	a cookbook
a romantic novel	a reference book
a detective story	a dictionary
science fiction	an encyclopedia

Exercise 2

1 *It's part of a bibliography. You'd find it at the back of a non-fiction book.*
2 It's part of an index. You'd find it at the back of a non-fiction book.
3 It's a verse from a poem.
4 It's the beginning of a chapter in a novel.
5 It's part of a contents page. You'd find it at the beginning of a non-fiction book.
6 It's part of an introduction to a non-fiction book.

Exercise 3a

1 *a poet*
2 a novelist / an author / a writer
3 a playwright / dramatist
4 a biographer
5 a textbook writer
6 a translator
7 a literary agent
8 a publisher
9 an editor
10 a printer

Exercise 4
Possible answers

1 an English dramatist: Shakespeare
an American novelist: J D Salinger
a poet who writes in English: Philip Larkin
a twentieth-century writer of short stories: Angela Carter
a writer of thrillers: Tom Clancy

11 Art

Exercise 1a

1 *painter*
2 picture
3 brush
4 palette
5 easel
6 canvas
7 photograph
8 camera
9 paints
10 frame

Exercise 1b

1 *an oil painting*
2 a sketch
3 a watercolour
4 a landscape
5 a still life
6 a portrait

Exercise 2

1 *painting; a painting; paint*
2 sculpture; a sculpture; marble, wood, metal, clay, porcelain
3 photography; a photo(graph); a (digital) camera, film, a flash, a dark room
4 ceramics; a ceramic, e.g. a pot; clay, porcelain

Exercise 3

1 *romantic*
2 impressionist
3 classical
4 cubist
5 abstract
6 surrealist

Exercise 4

Part A: How artistic are you?

Score 1 point for every tick in the *yes* column.
Score 1 point for every tick in the *at school* column.
Score 2 points for every tick in the *at home* column.
Maximum score: 60 points

Part B: What do you know about art?

1 The Mona Lisa. Leonardo da Vinci 2 points

2 1 c
  2 d
  3 g
  4 f
  5 b
  6 h
  7 a
  8 e
  8 points

Total: 70 points

Exercise 5

Possible answer

This is a surrealist painting by René Magritte. In the foreground is an easel with a painting of a landscape on it. The easel is in front of a window, which could look out onto the same landscape. There are curtains on the left- and right-hand sides of the picture.

12 The environment

Exercise 1

1 *a hurricane*
2 a volcano
3 a flood
4 an earthquake
5 a forest fire
6 an avalanche
7 a drought
8 a tornado

Exercise 2

1 Evacuate the area
2 Airlift people who are stuck in their houses to safety.
3 Build shelters on high ground.
4 Fly in emergency supplies.
5 Raise funds to help people rebuild their lives.

Exercise 3

E	X	H	A	U	S	T		I	C	E
X		Y		N			O	N		N
T	I	D	A	L		R	O	U	N	D
I		R		E		N				A
N		O	S	A	K	A		P	E	N
C	O			D			E			G
T		O		E	C	O	T	H	E	
I		P		D			R		R	
O		E				O	Z	O	N	E
N	U	C	L	E	A	R		L		D

Exercise 4

1 f (carbon dioxide)
2 j (toxic waste)
3 b (the greenhouse effect)
4 i *(nuclear waste)*
5 c (forest fires)
6 d (exhaust fumes)
7 h (global warming)
8 a (the ozone layer)
9 g (acid rain)
10 e (green issues)

1 *nuclear waste*
2 forest fires
3 exhaust fumes
4 acid rain
5 toxic waste

Exercise 5b

1 *F*
2 T
3 T
4 F (Scientists say temperatures could rise by up to another 8°C over the next 100 years.)
5 T
6 F (This temperature rise could mean more droughts, flooding, storms and higher sea levels.)
7 F (Politicians tend to focus on what will win them votes in six months' time, not what the world will be like in 20 or 30 years …)
8 T (I chaired the Youth Environment Conference…)
9 F (More than 170 fourteen- to twenty-five-year-olds turned up…)
10 F (But what concerned us most was how we can make a difference.)

Exercise 5c

Pollution

global warming, rising levels of carbon dioxide, greenhouse gases ....

Weather conditions

flooding, droughts, frequent storms ....

Effects on the environment

temperature rise, higher sea levels, ice caps could melt, (could) flood low-lying countries ....

Fuel	**Green energy**	**Other environmentally friendly ideas**
fossil fuel, coal	wind power	
petroleum	hydro-electric power	recycling schemes ....

Test yourself 3 (Units 9 to 12)

Exercise 1

0 *a ceramicist*
1 a painter
2 a photographer
3 a sculptor
4 an illustrator

0 *a biographer*
5 a novelist
6 a poet
7 a playwright / a dramatist
8 a motoring correspondent
9 a consumer affairs correspondent / editor
10 a foreign correspondent

Exercise 2

Possible answers

five more things a painter might use:
a sketch pad, an easel, a (paint)brush, paints,
a palette, pen and ink

**three more works of art a painter
might produce:**
a watercolour, an oil painting, a pastel, a portrait, a
landscape, a still life

two more things a photographer might use:
a dark room, a (digital) camera, film, a flash

Exercise 3

0 *based*
1 science
2 thriller
3 set
4 character
5 theme

Exercise 4

Possible answers

0 *the travel section,* home news, world news, features,
business, financial, arts, sports, obituaries, fashion, travel,
horoscopes, letters, weather forecast, gossip column,
crossword, cartoons, competition, listings, classified
advertisements, TV and radio listings, book / theatre / film
reviews, editorial / leader

Exercise 5

Possible answers

1 *acts* (and) scenes
2 chapters
3 verses
4 tabloid
5 comic
6 listings
7 weekly
8 reviews
9 editorial

Exercise 6

0 *effect*
1 warming
2 rain
3 layer
4 waste
5 destruction
6 sources
7 power
8 farms
9 fossil
10 group
11 warrior
12 recycle
13 fumes
14 petrol
15 diesel
16 environmental

The political spectrum

right wing .... extreme left / right
left wing ....
in the centre .... the left / right wing of the party
centre-left / left of centre ....
.... on the left / right
centre-right / right of centre ....
....

Elections

Verb phrases

run / stand for Parliament
....

go to the polls
....

be neck and neck in the polls
....

vote for (someone)
....

elect (someone)
....

hold an election / a referendum
....

campaign (for a party / candidate)
....

be in power
....

Noun phrases

vote ....
voter ....
floating voter ....
candidate ....
general election ....
local election ....
referendum ....
campaign ....
campaign slogan ....
opinion poll ....
constituency ....
seat ....
(= a constituency where there is an election)
proportional representation
....

> A **floating voter** is someone who does not always vote for the same party. Under the **first past the post system**, a candidate is elected by a simple majority, and the party which wins the most seats (that is, parliamentary constituencies) becomes the party of government. A **safe seat** describes a constituency where there is a large majority of people who vote for one particular party.

Political protest

(_ shows where the stress falls)

Verb	Noun (activity)	Noun (person)
d<u>e</u>monstrate	demon<u>stra</u>tion	d<u>e</u>monstrator
....	....	....
pro<u>test</u>	<u>pro</u>test	prot<u>e</u>stor
....	....	....
cam<u>paign</u>	cam<u>paign</u>	cam<u>paign</u>er
....	....	....
march	march	<u>march</u>er
....	....	....

REF

See page 85 for information about the British and US governments.

See pages 86 – 87 for the British / American word list.

7

1 Match each word in column A with a word from column B.

A   **B**

1 Prime   a election
2 Vice   b slogan
3 opinion   c Minister
4 proportional d poll
5 civil   e President
6 campaign   f representation
7 general   g servant
8 government   h minister

1 .....c..... Prime Minister
2 ....
3 ....
4 ....
5 ....
6 ....
7 ....
8 ....

2 Complete the captions.

Name	Nero	Queen Elizabeth II	Franco
Status			dictator
System	empire	monarchy	

Name	Margaret Thatcher	Tony Blair	George Bush
Status			
Political Party	Conservative	Labour	

3 Try this quiz. The answers are in the POLITICS wordsearch.

Quiz: How much do you know about politics?

This person

1 is based at the town hall and represents his / her town or city.
   mayor ....

2 is a country's principal representative in another country.
   ....

3 is one of several people who represents his / her country in another country. ....

4 works in a government department, helping MPs with their work.
   ....

5 wants to be chosen for government.
   ....

6 votes sometimes for one party, sometimes for another.
   ....

7 goes into the streets, with others, to protest about government policy.
   ....

8 works to get a politician elected.
   ....

What do you call

9 a survey of voters' views?
   ....

10 the occasion when people choose who they want to represent them?
   ....

11 the occasion when people vote on a particular subject?
   ....

12 a government which is made up of representatives of more than one party? ....

How would you describe their political philosophy?

13 "The state should control everything, and there should be no different social classes." ....

14 "Market forces, profit and private enterprise are what matter."
   ....

15 "Everyone should have equal opportunities to share in the wealth of the state." ....

L	U	D	R	E	P	C	O	A	L	I	T	I	O	N
E	F	L	O	A	T	I	N	G	V	O	T	E	R	U
C	A	M	P	A	I	G	N	E	R	T	M	Y	O	R
A	P	C	I	V	I	L	S	E	R	V	A	N	T	E
N	M	S	N	T	O	M	O	L	J	C	M	T	L	F
D	R	W	I	P	B	U	C	E	P	W	B	V	C	E
I	R	P	O	L	I	T	I	C	S	M	A	Y	O	R
D	E	H	N	R	S	P	A	T	D	O	S	L	M	E
A	C	A	P	I	T	A	L	I	S	T	S	O	M	N
T	A	R	O	L	H	U	I	O	P	J	A	P	U	D
E	E	P	L	R	Y	L	S	N	Y	E	D	I	N	U
D	I	P	L	O	M	A	T	T	N	C	O	X	I	M
D	E	M	O	N	S	T	R	A	T	O	R	L	S	E
I	T	U	E	W	E	N	A	K	P	S	W	R	T	L

Check your answers on page D.

7

4a Put these labels in the correct places on the spectrum.

centre	extreme left	right of centre	extreme right
left of centre	right wing	left wing	

1 *extreme left*   2 ....   3 ....   4 ....   5 ....

6 ....   7 ....

4b Write *me* to show where you are on the spectrum. Then add the names of some politicians you know to the spectrum.

5 Complete this extract from a politician's autobiography, using the words in the box.

campaign	candidates	held	slogan	party	vote
seat	election	wing	neck	neck	stood

The 2001 Election

I ¹ *stood* for Parliament in the 2001 general ²............................ .
There were five ³............................ altogether. It was a long and hard
⁴............................ . Our ⁵............................ was *A real chance for a real change.*

The election was ⁶............................ on Thursday 7th June. The previous
week, my main rival and I were ⁷............................ and ⁸............................ in
the polls. But by Tuesday 5th, it was clear that most people would
⁹............................ for her, even though she's on the right ¹⁰............................
of her ¹¹............................ . They did, and she won the ¹²............................ .

6 Read about Cuba and Finland. Then give similar information about your country.

CUBA	
1 location	Cuba is an island in the Caribbean.
2 political system political parties opposition	It is a communist republic, a one-party state in which people do not have the right to demonstrate or to organize political opposition.
3 elections voting	You have the right to vote at the age of 16 if you are employed; otherwise, the voting age is 18.
FINLAND	
1 location	Finland has borders with Sweden, Norway and Russia.
2 political system political parties opposition	It is a democratic republic. Political parties include the Social Democratic Party, the National Coalition Party, the Centre Party and the Left-Wing Alliance.
3 elections voting	Elections are held every four years. Finland has a proportional representation voting system, which means that it usually has coalition governments. The voting age is 18. Finland was the first country in Europe to give women the right to vote (1906).
....	
1 location	
2 political system political parties opposition	
3 elections voting	

7 Write ten words and five expressions you are going to memorize.

Words	Expressions
1	1 ....
2	....
3	2 ....
4	....
5	3 ....
6	....
7	4 ....
8	....
9	5 ....
10	....

The law and crime

Translate the words and phrases.

Locations

police station	....
court	....
courtroom	....
prison	....

People connected with the law

the police	....
police officer	....
detective	....
solicitor	....
lawyer	....
barrister	....

In court

magistrate	....
trial	....
judge	....
jury	....
member of the jury	....
chairman of the jury	....
the prosecution	....
the defence	....
the defendant / accused	....
witness	....
victim	....

Breaking the law

It's against the law to drink and drive.

....

It's illegal to get a tattoo if you're under 18.

....

It's illegal for children under 16 to buy fireworks.

....

The government has imposed a curfew.

....

Crimes and criminals

burglary	....	burglar	....
theft	....	thief (plural: thieves)	....
(armed) robbery	....	(armed) robber	....
assault	....	assailant	....
manslaughter	....	killer	....
murder	....	murderer	....
fraud	....	fraudster	....
shoplifting	....	shoplifter	....
joy riding	....	joy rider	....
mugging	....	mugger	....
drug dealing	....	drug dealer	....

He broke into a house.

....

He stole some money.

....

He committed (murder, assault).

....

He was arrested.

....

He was taken into custody.

....

He was fingerprinted.

....

He was charged with (murder).

....

He was sent for trial.

....

He was on trial for (murder).

....

He appeared in court.

....

He pleaded guilty / not guilty.

....

His neighbours gave evidence against him.

....

What was the jury's verdict?

....

The jury found him guilty / not guilty.

....

He said he was innocent.

....

He was convicted of (manslaughter).

....

He got into trouble with the police.

....

He got caught driving without a licence.

....

He was banned from driving for two years.

....

He's now got a criminal record.

....

He got away with it.*

....

They let him off.*

....

Expressions marked * are used in informal, conversational language.

Sentences

He did 100 hours of community service.

....

He went to a young offenders' institution.

....

He went to prison.

....

He was sentenced to three years in prison.

....

He got a life sentence.

....

He got a suspended sentence.

....

He was locked up.

....

He was fined.

....

He got a heavy fine.

....

He went down for three years.*

....

He got done for robbery.*

....

He did time for burglary.*

....

He got life.*

....

REF See page 87 for the British / American word list.

1a Who are these people?

My court deals with criminal cases like shoplifting and vandalism.

I advise people when they're buying a house, having a dispute with neighbours and things like that.

1 *a magistrate*............... 2 ....

I spend some time at the station, some time in a car and some time walking around my local neighbourhood.

I represent people in the High Court.

My job is to find information which will help to bring criminals to justice.

3 .... 4 .... 5 ....

1b Who's talking?

| a witness | the defendant | the prosecution |
| the defence | the judge | the chairman of the jury |

1 'We find the defendant guilty.'   *the chairman of the jury*

2 'How do you plead? Guilty or not guilty?'   ....

3 'I saw the accused enter the house in Mill Street at about 7.30 p.m.'   ....

4 'I was not in Mill Street at 7.30. I was at home.'   ....

5 'It is clear that the accused was not in Mill Street and could not therefore have committed the crime.'   ....

6 'The accused cannot prove that he was at home all evening on the date in question.'   ....

2 Number these sentences to show the order in which the events occurred.

- ☐ He drove home.
- ☐ He pleaded guilty.
- ☐ He was charged with drink driving.
- ☐ He was fined and banned from driving for two years.
- ☐ He appeared in court.
- ☐ He was stopped by the police.
- ☐ 1 He went to the pub with his friends on his eighteenth birthday.
- ☐ They arrested him.

3 Solve the crossword.

Across ►

1 It's ... the law to travel on public transport without a ticket. (7)

4 You are ... trial for armed robbery. (2)

6 Unfortunately, there were ... witnesses. (2)

8 The ...room is where a trial takes place. (5)

9 Two teenagers have been arrested for joy-... . (6)

10 Obvious (5)

11 Did she ... time for shoplifting? (2)

13 She appeared ... court. (2)

14 The crime which a thief commits. (5)

15 She was convicted ... assault. (2)

Down ▼

1 She was charged with assault ... burglary. (3)

2 It's ... offence to deal in drugs. (2)

3 She was ... to two years in prison. (9)

5 ... is a more serious crime than manslaughter. (6)

7 Not guilty. (8)

8 A law stating times when people must be indoors. (6)

12 The magistrate let him ... with a warning. (3)

13 She wasn't convicted of the crime. She got away with ... . (2)

8

4a In column A, write down what you think the missing age is.

4b Check your answers on page E. Write the correct age in the text.

	A		**B**
	Age?	The law in Britain	In my country
1	*13*	At *13* you can earn money from a part-time job. You can only work a maximum of two hours on school days, two hours on Sundays, five hours on Saturdays and 25 hours a week during school holidays. The job must be 'light work' (not something like road building).	
2		At . . . you can work full-time.	
3		From the age of . . . you can be convicted of a criminal offence. (In Scotland, it is 8 at present but will soon be raised to 12.)	
4		At . . . you can be sent to a young offenders' institution.	
5		At . . . you can serve on a jury.	
6		At . . . you can go to a pub but you can only have soft drinks.	
7		At . . . you can buy and drink alcohol in a pub.	
8		At . . . you can buy a pet without having an adult with you.	
9		At . . . you can buy cigarettes and tobacco, fireworks and lottery tickets.	
10		At . . . you can vote in local or general elections.	
11		At . . . you can drive a moped.	
12		At . . . you can learn to drive a car.	
13		At . . . you can get a tattoo.	
14		At . . . girls can join the Armed Forces.	
15		At . . . boys can join certain sections of the Armed Forces without their parents' permission.	
16		At . . . you can leave school on the last Friday in June.	
17		At . . . you can leave home (if your parents agree).	
18		At . . . you can get married (with your parents' permission in England and Wales; without in Scotland).	
19		At . . . you can leave home and marry even if parents don't agree.	
20		At . . . you can adopt children.	

Source: T2, The Daily Telegraph

4c In column B, write the corresponding ages in your country and make a brief note of any differences. (If you are working in class, share the information.)

5 What do you think should happen to children and teenagers who break the law? Read Sharon Moore's opinion of the law in Britain. Then write a paragraph about your country and give your opinions.

> *You can be locked up at 10, but you can't buy a pet until you're 12, get married until you're 16 or vote until you're 18. The age of criminal responsibility in the UK is too low and should be raised to at least 12. In Turkey it is 12; in Belgium and Luxembourg it's 18. Most other European countries fall somewhere in between. We want an end to prison custody for under-18s.*
>
> Sharon Moore, Youth Justice Programme Manager at the Children's Society

....
....
....
....
....

6 Write ten words and five expressions you are going to memorize.

Words	Expressions
1	1 ....
2	....
3	2 ....
4	....
5	3 ....
6	....
7	4 ....
8	....
9	5 ....
10	....

Test yourself 2 (Units 5 to 8)

How much can you remember?

My mark: _____
60

1 What do you need in order to

0   have a shower?

some shower gel ....

1   have a wash?

....

2   wash your hair?

....

and ....

3   clean your teeth?

....

and ....

4   shave?

....

and ....

5   cut your nails?

....

(8 marks)

2 Put the words into the correct categories.

ache	diabetes	kidneys	stiffness
asthma	heart	liver	stomach
brain	hepatitis	lungs	tenderness
cholera	irritation	pain	typhoid

Internal organs	Illnesses and diseases	Physical sensations and states
0 *brain*		
1	6	11 ....
2	7	12 ....
3	8	13 ....
4	9	14 ....
5	10	15 ....

(15 marks)

3 Write two more examples of

1 social events: *a get-together* ...., ..., ...

2 special interest groups: *a theatre group* ...., ...

3 social issues: *drug addiction* ...., ..., ...

4 systems of government: *monarchy* ...., ..., ...

5 social classes in Britain   *the upper class* ...., ..., ...

(10 marks)

4 Complete what they are saying.

0 "You have the _right_ .... to vote, so use it!"

1 "The government wants to introduce .... cards, which will have your name, date of birth and fingerprints on them."

2 "We must be allowed to say what we think. We must have .... of speech."

3 "The most important issue for me is .... and order."

4 "This government has been in .... for ten years, and it's time for a change."

5 "The government can do what it wants, because the .... is so weak."

6 "The latest opinion .... shows that the government is as popular as ever."

7 "I don't think the generation .... is getting bigger. I think it's getting smaller."

(7 marks)

5 What do you call someone who

0	obtains money by pretending to be someone else?	_a fraudster_ ....
1	breaks into a house?	....
2	kills someone?	....
3	steals from someone?	....
4	arrests a criminal?	....
5	investigates crimes?	....
6	sees a crime as it is happening?	....
7	is robbed or hurt in an assault?	....
8	is the head of the jury in court?	....
9	asks the head of the jury for the jury's decision?	....
10	represents in court the person who is accused of a crime?	....

(10 marks)

6 Complete the following account.

Jason Rowlands
Crime Correspondent

On Thursday 12th July, a thief broke 0 _into_ .... a house in Lynton Road and stole TV, audio and computer equipment worth £25,000. Two weeks later, Barry Turner, a self-employed electrician who lives a few streets away, in Torbay Avenue, was arrested by the police and 1 .... into custody. Fingerprints taken at the scene of the crime matched those of Turner, who was 2 .... with burglary. Turner claimed that he was 3 .... He had been at the house in Lynton Road doing some electrical repairs, which is why his fingerprints were there. However, Turner's neighbours gave 4 .... against him, saying that he had offered to sell them TVs, hi-fis and computer equipment in late July. Turner was therefore sent for 5 .... He appeared in 6 .... last week. He 7 .... not guilty. The 8 .... took two days to reach a 9 ...., but eventually found him guilty. Turner was 10 .... to three months in prison.

(10 marks)

9 Newspapers and magazines

Translate the words and phrases.

The press

newspaper / paper	....
national newspaper	....
local newspaper	....
(fashion) magazine	....
satirical magazine	....
(scientific) journal	....
comic	....
listings magazine	....

fanzine	....
e-zine	....

> A **fanzine** is a magazine for fans of a pop group or sports team. An **e-zine** is a magazine which appears on the Internet.

a daily newspaper

....

a weekly / fortnightly / monthly magazine

....

> British newspapers are either **broadsheets** or **tabloids**. A broadsheet is a large-format newspaper, a 'quality newspaper' with a higher intellectual content than a tabloid. A tabloid is a small-format newspaper featuring short news items, stories about famous people and sensational stories.

a broadsheet

a tabloid

People

editor	....
reporter	....
reviewer	....
journalist	....

... correspondent / editor

foreign	....
crime	....
fashion	....
social affairs	....
economics	....
motoring	....
political	....
medical	....
arts	....
consumer affairs	....
travel	....

sports reporter	....
book reviewer	....
photographer	....
designer	....
illustrator	....
cartoonist	....

Departments

editorial	....
design	....
advertising	....
production	....

> REF
>
> See also page 18, Unit 3 (Company departments).

Sections of a newspaper

home news	....	cartoons	....
world news	....	competition	....
features	....	listings	....
business	....	classified advertisements	
financial	....		....
arts	....	TV and radio listings	
sports	....		....
obituaries	....	book / theatre / film reviews	
fashion	....		....
travel	....		
horoscopes	....	editorial / leader	
letters	....		....
weather forecast	....		
gossip column	....	
crossword	....	

> An **editorial** or **leader**, usually found on the inside pages, gives the editor's opinion on current events, rather than reporting them.

Features of a page

headline	....
column	....
caption	....
advertisement / advert / ad	....
an article about ...	
....	
a report on ...	
....	
a feature on ...	
....	
an exclusive interview with ...	
....	

It's nice to see Tracy taking an interest in the news.

The Sun is Britain's most popular tabloid newspaper.

....

What are the circulation figures?

....

It sells three and a half million copies a day.

....

I've taken out a subscription to *Smash Hits*.

....

I don't read a magazine from cover to cover. I dip into it.

....

Value judgements

fair	....
balanced	....
biased	....
boring	....
entertaining	....
intrusive	....
sensationalist	....

REF

> See page 87 for the British / American word list.

1a Complete the words for people who work on newspapers and magazines.

	Articles	Visuals		Articles	Visuals
1 j o urnal i s t	✓		5 r _ v _ _ wer		
2 photo _ _ _ _ _ _ _ _			6 _ ll _ st _ _ tor		
3 r _ p _ _ ter			7 c _ rt _ _ n _ st		
4 d _ s _ _ ner			8 c _ rr _ _ p _ _ dent		

1b Which of them write the articles? Which of them deal with the visual aspects? Tick the correct columns above.

2a Think of an example of each of the following in your country (or in Britain). Write the title.

1 a national newspaper ....
2 a local newspaper ....
3 a fashion magazine ....
4 a music magazine ....
5 a satirical magazine ....
6 a listings magazine ....
7 a special interest (e.g. football) magazine ....
8 a fanzine ....
9 a scientific journal ....
10 a comic ....

2b Give an example of a newspaper in your country which is similar to

1 a broadsheet ....
2 a tabloid ....

3 Try this competition.

COMPETITION: So you want to be a journalist?

Win a day with the editors at top teen magazine *Sugar*!

❶ Which is the most popular newspaper in your country?..................
● What are the circulation figures?
....
● Which is the most popular magazine?
....

❷ Would you prefer to work on a newspaper or a magazine? ....
● Why?..................
....
● In which department would you like to work?..................
● What would you like to be? ....
....
● Why?..................
....

❸ How do you read your magazine?
☐ From cover to cover. ☐ I dip into it.

❹ You've just got a job writing for your favourite magazine (*Sugar*, of course!). What would you write about, and who would you interview?

I'd write a report on ....
....
I'd write a feature on ....
....
I'd do an exclusive interview with ....
....

4a Which of these descriptions are positive and which are negative? Write them in the correct group.

balanced	intrusive	sensationalist
biased	entertaining	fair

☺ *balanced* ....

....

....

☹ ....

....

....

4b Which of the words in 4a would you use to describe the following?

CAUGHT ON CAMERA *EXCLUSIVE!*

THE PICTURES THE FAMOUS WOULD RATHER YOU DIDN'T SEE SEE PAGE 18

1 ....

EXPOSED: FOOD SCANDAL IN OUR RESTAURANTS

2 ....

THE CASE FOR ...

AND AGAINST

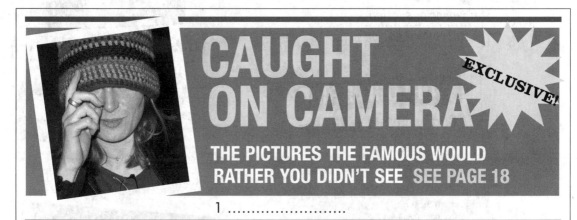

First cow: MOO!
Second cow: BAA!
First cow: What do you mean BAA!?
Second cow: I'm learning a foreign language!

3 ....

4 ....

9

5a Which sections of the newspaper are these extracts from?

5b Who is responsible for them?

─── Money matters ───

Rich banks rob the poor

WE'VE suspected it for many years, but the true extent of the interest rate rip-off on High Street savers is astonishing. In most years since 1980, High Street savers in instant access

1 a *the financial section*
  b *the economics editor*

How the cardigan became cool

While drawing the line at the belted variety, aficionados of style are taking

5 a ....
  b ....

WORLD IN BRIEF

Curfew in Sri Lanka after election shock

Police reimposed a curfew throughout Sri Lanka last night as the victorious opposition alliance prepared to form a government in consultation with President Chandrika Kumaratunga

2 a ....
  b ....

Escape — Ethiopia reveals its treasures

3 a ....
  b ....

WORTHY WINNERS

Spurs joy

6 a ....
  b ....

Two arrested in robbery

Two men in their early 30s were arrested yesterday by police in Guildford in connection with a theft from a jeweller's

4 a ....
  b ....

Bikes on trial

The best bikes for under £250

The number one choice

the TMX trekker

7 a ....
  b ....

6 What are these extracts from?

1 _a weather forecast_ ....

Sandra Bartlett

forecasts what's in the stars for you tomorrow

2 ....

PRIZES TO WIN

4 ....

THE LORD OF THE RINGS

Technically wonderful – but oh so monotonous

PEOPLE in the Lord Of Th Rings have more hair than they do in

3 ....

Under-18s shouldn't go to war

The Government has been criticised for allowing under-18s to fight in conflicts. This newspaper believes that under-18s should

5 ....

DAVID ASTOR: 1912–2001

6 ....

7 In exercises 5 and 6, find an example of

1 a headline ....

2 a picture caption ....

8 Write ten words and five expressions you are going to memorize.

Words	Expressions
1	1 ....
2	....
3	2 ....
4	....
5	3 ....
6	....
7	4 ....
8	....
9	5 ....
10	....

10 Books

Translate the words and phrases.

Literature

fiction	....	play	....
non-fiction	....	poem	....

Fiction

novel	....	short story	....
romantic novel	....	ghost story	....
historical novel	....	detective story	....
contemporary novel	....	science fiction	....
thriller	....		

Non–fiction

reference book	....	cookbook	....
atlas	....	instruction manual	....
dictionary	....	textbook	....
encyclopedia	....	autobiography	....
travel book	....	biography	....
guidebook	....		

People

writer	....	literary agent	....
author	....	translator	....
novelist	....	editor	....
poet	....	publisher	....
playwright / dramatist	....	printer	....
biographer	....	audience	....
textbook writer	....	readership	....

Book covers

paperback	....	front / back cover	....
hardback	....	blurb	....
jacket	....		

The **blurb** is a short description on the jacket or back cover of a book. It tells you what the book is about.

Divisions

Fiction

chapter ....

Poem

verse ....
line ....

Play

act ....
scene ....

Non-fiction

contents ....
introduction ....
notes ....
bibliography ....
index ....

Elements of fiction

story ....
plot ....
narrative ....
character ....
hero / heroine ....
scene ....
setting ....
theme ....
ending ....

What are you writing?
My autobiography.
What's it about?

Talking about books

It's a book by J K Rowling.
....

It's called *Harry Potter*.
....

It's about …
....

It's set in …
....

It's for children, but it also appeals to adults.
....

It's been translated into …
....

It's been made into a film.
....

The plot of *Great Expectations* is quite complicated.
....

The dialogue is really good.
....

The main character is a boy called Pip.
....

There are two main themes: love and selfishness.
....

Is it based on a true story?
....

I read it in translation.
....

It's an exciting story.
....

I couldn't put it down!
....

It's a classic.
....

REF
See page 87 for the British / American word list.

1a Write the jumbled words correctly. They are all types of book.

1 **promocenatry** a novel .....contemporary.......

2 an **alsta** ....

3 a **trosh** story ....

4 a **gotsh** story ....

5 a **grabiophy** ....

6 a **rillerth** ....

7 a **vartel** book ....

8 a **choristial** novel ....

9 a **deguikoob** ....

10 a **koobkooc** ....

11 a **ferenecer** book ....

12 a **tricidonay** ....

13 a **trimonac** novel ....

14 a **veticedet** story ....

15 an **apilocendyce** ....

16 **siccene tificon** ....

1b Put the words in 1a into the correct group.

Fiction		Non-fiction	
a contemporary novel..	☐	....	☐
....	☐	....	☐
....	☐	....	☐
....	☐	....	☐
....	☐	....	☐
....	☐	....	☐
....	☐	....	☐
		....	☐

1c Tick the ones you have read or used recently.

2 What are these and where would you find them?

> *Archaeological Sites of the Lake District,* T. Clare (Moorland Publishing Co., 1981)
> *A Complete Guide to the English Lakes,* Harriet Martineau (John Garnett, Windermere, 1855)
> *A Concise Description of the English Lakes,* Jonathan Otley (P by the author, Keswick, 1823)

> **4**
> I arrived at Felicity's house, Passmore, 1006 Divine Road midnight. The United Airlines Heathrow-Boston flight v – I was on standby, I had the *will-I-fly, wont-I-fly?* in

1 *It's part of a bibliography. You'd find it at the back of a non-fiction book.*

4 ....

....

> earthquake, *see* San Francisco
> East India Company, British, 26
> Eastman, George, American inventor, 12
> Edison, Thomas, American inventor, 12-13, **13**, 52
> education; Britain and United States, 16, **17**; in India, 2

> 4   Western Society
> 6   France: the Golden Years
> 8   Fashion
> 10 Suffragettes
> 12 Science and Daily Life

2 ....

....

5 ....

....

> I walked last night with my old friend
> Past the old house where we first met,
> Past each known bush and each known bend.
> The moon shone, and the path was wet.

> **The early cinema**
> *One of the most important changes to people's lives at the beginning of the twentieth century was the introduction of the cinema*

3 ....

....

6 ....

....

3a Who are these people?

1 (I write poetry.) 2 (I write novels.) 3 (I write plays.) 4 (I write books about people's lives.)

..........*a poet*..........   ....

....

5 (I write books for schools.) 6 (I change the language of a book, e.g. from English to French.) 7 (I help authors find someone to publish their books.)

....

8 (Number 7 comes to me with ideas for books.) 9 (I work for number 8. I check the text of a book.) 10 (Number 9 hands a book to me to make lots of copies.)

....

3b Which of the people in 3a would you like to be? Why?

4 Try this questionnaire.

1 Can you name
- an English dramatist?
  ....
- an American novelist?
  ....
- a poet who writes in English?
  ....
- a twentieth-century writer of short stories?
  ....
- a writer of thrillers?
  ....

2 In the last year, how many novels or short stories have you read?
  a) More than 6 ☐
  b) 1–5 ☐
  c) 0 ☐

3 Have you ever read
- a historical novel?
  Yes ☐ No ☐ Title.................................
- a biography?
  Yes ☐ No ☐ Title.................................

- an autobiography?
  Yes ☐ No ☐ Title.............................
- a book in translation?
  Yes ☐ No ☐ Title.............................
- a play in English?
  Yes ☐ No ☐ Title.........................

4 When you get a new piece of equipment like a computer or a watch, do you
  a) read the instruction
     manual first? ☐
  b) dip into the instruction manual
     when you run into problems? ☐
  c) ignore the instruction manual
     completely? ☐

5

Which of the following do you use regularly?
- A dictionary ☐
- An atlas ☐
- An encyclopedia ☐

5 Think of a book you've read (or a film you've seen). Make notes in the chart. Then write a paragraph about it.

Title ....
Author ....
Setting (place?) ....
Time (e.g. the 1950s) ....
Readership (children? teenagers? adults?)..
Main characters (names? relationship to each other?)..
Based on a true story?...
Theme(s) (love? growing up? loyalty?)..
Ending (exciting? disappointing?)..
Opinion ....

Books and you

6 Can you remember two lines from a poem (in any language)? Yes ☐ No ☐
If 'yes', what are they?

....

....

....

7 When you go to a country where the language is not your first language, do you take

a) a guidebook, a phrasebook and a dictionary? ☐

b) two of the above? ☐

c) none of the above? ☐

8 Can you name three books which you would describe as *classics*?

1 ....

2 ....

3 ....

9 How often do you read a book for pleasure (that is, not because you have to)?

a) all the time ☐

b) occasionally ☐

c) never ☐

10 Have you ever written a story, a poem or a play?

a) Yes, I've written all three. ☐

b) Yes, I've written one of them. ☐

c) Yes, when I was at primary school. ☐

Analysis

1		2		3		4		5		6		7		8		9		10	
four to five answers	3	a)	3	all five	3	a)	3	all three	3	yes	3	a)	3	three	3	a)	3	a)	3
two to three answers	2	b)	2	one to four	2	b)	2	one or two	2	no	0	b)	2	one or two	2	b)	2	b)	2
one answer	1	c)	0	none	0	c)	1	none	0			c)	1	none	0	c)	0	c)	1
no answers	0																		

25–30 points Wow! You read a lot. And if your answer to Question 10 was *a)*, then maybe it's time you found a literary agent. But don't spend all your time with books. The real world's out there waiting for you …

11–24 points Well done! Will you go on to study literature or languages?

3–10 points You're probably better at sciences than arts and literature.

---

6 Write ten words and five expressions you are going to memorize.

Words	Expressions
1	1 ....
2	....
3	2 ....
4	....
5	3 ....
6	....
7	4 ....
8	....
9	5 ....
10	....

11 Art

Translate the words and phrases.

Person		Activity	
artist	....	(create)	....
designer	....	design	....
painter	....	paint	....
sculptor	....	sculpt	....
photographer	....	photograph	....
illustrator	....	/ take a photo	....
ceramicist	....	illustrate	....
		make ceramics / pots	....

*She's on an assignment. She's **photographing** wildlife in Madagascar. (She's doing it professionally.)*
*We **took photos** of some of the animals when we went to the zoo. (We're not professional photographers.)*

Works of art

a painting*	....	a (black and white / colour) photo(graph)**	
a drawing*	....	....	
an oil painting	....	a ceramic**, e.g. a pot	
a watercolour	....	....	
a pastel	....		
a sketch	....	She paints landscapes.	
a portrait	....	....	
a landscape	....	I'll just do a quick sketch.	
a still life	....	....	
an original	....		
a print	....		
a copy	....		
a design*	....		
a sculpture*	....		
an illustration*	....		

> **Works of art** marked * are also used as
> uncountable nouns to describe types of art which
> can be studied or specialized in, e.g. I specialize
> in sculpture. I'm studying design. Those marked **
> change form when used in this way: photography,
> ceramics, e.g. I'm interested in photography.

Art equipment and materials

paint (*uncountable*)	....	pen and ink	....
paints (*plural*)	....	(paint)brush	....
oils	....	easel	....
acrylics / acrylic paints	....	palette	....
watercolours	....	sketch pad	....
pastels	....	canvas	....
charcoal	....	frame	....
She works in oils.		She specializes in watercolours.	

....

Styles of painting (adjectives)

classical ....
romantic ....
impressionist ....
surrealist ....
cubist ....
realistic ....
naturalistic ....
figurative ....
abstract ....
graphic ....
Renaissance ....

> The corresponding nouns / noun phrases for **styles of painting** are:
>
> classicism   cubism   abstract art
> romanticism   realism   graphic art
> impressionism   naturalism   Renaissance art
> surrealism   figurative art

Describing paintings

It's in the style of (Van Gogh).
In the …

        foreground …
....

        middle distance …
....

        background …
....

        top right- / left-hand corner …
....

        bottom right- / left-hand corner …
....

Sculpture and ceramics

marble ....
wood ....
metal ....
clay ....
porcelain ....

Photographic equipment and materials

(digital) camera ....
film ....
flash ....
negative ....
transparency ....
dark room ....
How many shots have you taken?

....

Have you had the film developed yet?

....

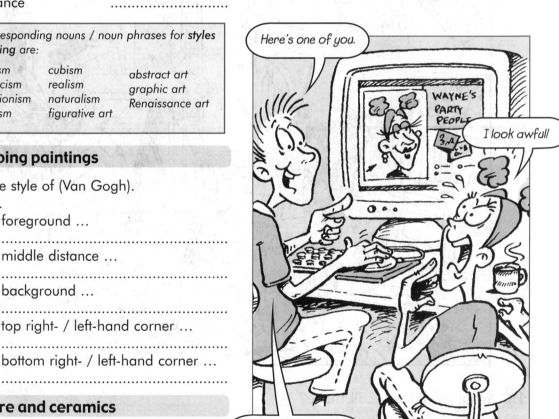

See also **Boost Your Vocabulary 3**, page 59, (Metals and other materials).

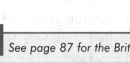

See page 87 for the British / American word list.

1a Label the picture.

2 pi.....................

1 pa*inter*.................

3 br.....................

4 pa.....................

5 ea.....................

6 ca.....................

7 ph.................

8 ca.....................

9 pa.................

10 fr.................

1b What would you call these?

1 A painting done in oil-based paints.

an oil painting..........................

2 A quick drawing, or a drawing you do in preparation for a painting.

....

3 A painting done in water-based paints.

....

4 A picture showing fields, trees and hills.

....

5 A picture of an arrangement of objects, such as flowers or fruit.

....

6 A picture of a person.

....

2 Complete the chart.

people	art / area of work	individual works of art	materials
1 a painter	*painting*	*a painting*	*paint*
2 a sculptor			
3 a photographer			
4 a ceramicist			

3 Use the words in the box to describe the style of these works of art.

- abstract
- classical
- cubist
- impressionist
- romantic
- surrealist

romantic

....

....

....

....

....

11

4 Try this quiz.

Part A: How artistic are you?

Tick the correct column.

Have you ever	yes	no	at school	at home
1 designed and made an object?				
2 used watercolours?				
3 used oils?				
4 used pastels?				
5 sketched in charcoal?				
6 used a sketch book?				
7 painted a portrait?				
8 painted a landscape?				
9 painted on canvas?				
10 drawn a cartoon?				
11 framed a picture?				
12 illustrated a poem?				
13 drawn plans for a building?				
14 taken an artistic photo?				
15 developed your own photos?				

5 Write a description of this picture. Use
- words to do with painting
- phrases / prepositions of place

How would you describe the style?

....
....
....
....
....
....
....

The Human Condition, 1 René Magritte, 1934

Part B: What do you know about art?

What is the most famous painting in the world? Who painted it?

....

They all begin with M, but can you match the artist to the description?

1	Buonarrotti **M**ichelangelo	....	**a**	a Belgian Surrealist painter
2	Claude **M**onet	....	**b**	a Dutch abstract painter
3	**M**an Ray	....	**c**	a Florentine Renaissance sculptor, painter and poet
4	Charles Rennie **M**ackintosh	....	**d**	a French Impressionist painter
5	Piet **M**ondrian	....	**e**	a Norwegian painter and print-maker
6	Henry **M**oore	....	**f**	a Scottish designer and architect
7	René **M**agritte	....	**g**	an American Surrealist photographer and film maker
8	Edvard **M**unch	....	**h**	an English sculptor

Go to page G to find out how you scored.

6 Write ten words and five expressions you are going to memorize.

Words	Expressions
1	1 ....
2	....
3	2 ....
4	....
5	3 ....
6	....
7	4 ....
8	....
9	5 ....
10	....

12 The environment

Translate the words and phrases.

Natural disasters

earthquake	....
volcanic eruption	....
hurricane	....
tornado, whirlwind	....
storm	....
drought	....
forest fire	....
avalanche	....
flood	....
tidal wave	....

Emergency help

Emergency supplies were flown in.
....

The area was evacuated.
....

People were airlifted to safety.
....

Shelters were built.
....

An international relief fund was started.
....

Aid was provided by some major charities.
....

Environmental pollution

exhaust fumes	....
toxic waste	....
chemicals	....
greenhouse gases	....
the greenhouse effect	....
global warming	....
carbon dioxide (CO_2)	....
the ozone layer	....
the atmosphere	....
acid rain	....

Effects

The ice caps are melting.
....

Sea levels are rising.
....

Low-lying areas are being flooded.
....

Animals and plants

The blue whale is an endangered species / is in danger of extinction.
....

The Indian elephant is a protected species.
....

The destruction of the rainforest is an ecological disaster.
....

We're studying the ecosystem of the rainforest.
....

Traditional sources of energy and fuel

fossil fuels	....
coal	....
gas	....
oil	....
petrol	....
diesel	....
nuclear power	....

Coal-fired power stations contribute to the greenhouse effect.
....

Nuclear power is used to generate electricity.
....

Alternative energy

solar power ....
hydro-electric power ....
wave power ....
water power ....
wind farms ....

Resources and energy

renewable energy sources

....
recycling centre ....
recycle ....
save energy ....
save water ....

Green products

green energy ....
unleaded petrol ....
recycled paper / glass ....
organic products (e.g. fruit and vegetables)

....

Food production

pesticides ....
fertilisers ....
organic farming ....
genetically modified (GM) crops

....

The environment and politics

pressure groups ....
environmental campaign ....
green issues ....
eco-warrior ....

Happy birthday, Lisa!

Oh, er, thanks, Tracy.

But I gave you that for your birthday!

I know. I just recycled it.

REF See page 87 for the British / American word list.

1 What are these natural disasters? Label the pictures.

a hurricane

....

....

....

....

....

....

....

2 A large area of your country is about to be flooded. In which order would you do the following things?

☐ Fly in emergency supplies.

☐ Raise funds to help people rebuild their lives.

☐ Airlift people who are stuck in their houses to safety.

☐ Evacuate the area.

☐ Build shelters on high ground.

3 Solve the crossword.

|1| |2| |3| |4| |5| |6|
10					11				
			12 O S A K A		13
14									
	15		16			17			
					18				
19									

Down ▼

1. The Indian elephant is in danger of … . (10)
2. …-electric power is another name for electricity produced by water power. (5)
3. Petrol without lead. (8)
4. Another word for whirlwind. (7)
6. An … species is one that is in danger of dying out. (10)
9. Organic farming uses … pesticides or fertilizers. (2)
13. Fuel for cars. (6)
15. Abbreviation for the Organization of Petroleum Exporting Countries. (4)
18. Which is cheaper, solar power … wind power? (2)

Across ▶

1. … fumes come from cars. (7)
5. Global warming will cause the … caps to melt. (3)
8. What is the effect of pollution … the atmosphere? (2)
10. A … wave is a huge wave of water. (5)
11. The shape of the hole in the ozone layer. (5)
12. The third largest city in Japan. (5)
13. Which is more environmentally friendly, a biro or a fountain …? (3)
14. ….$_2$ = carbon dioxide. (2)
16. An …-warrior is an environmental protester. (3)
17. Save … world! (3)
18. The … layer prevents harmful radiation from the sun reaching the Earth. (5)
19. … power stations were built to replace coal-fired power stations. (7)

4 Match each word in column A with a word in column B to make phrases. Then use five of the phrases to label the picture.

A		B	
1	carbon	a	layer
2	toxic	b	effect
3	the green-house	c	fires
		d	fumes
4	nuclear	e	issues
5	forest	f	dioxide
6	exhaust	g	rain
7	global	h	warming
8	the ozone	i	waste
9	acid	j	waste
10	green		

1 nuclear waste
2 ....
3 ....
4 ....
5 ....

1 ......   2 ......   3 ......   4 ..i..   5 ......
6 ......   7 ......   8 ......   9 ......   10......

5a Read the article from a teenage newspaper.

CAUSE ▶▶▶

EFFECT ▶▶▶

Tom Barton, 19, is studying politics at York University.

The past weeks have been dominated by the environment: fuel protests, severe flooding, a Government paper on green cities, and this week the global warming conference in The Hague.

But what is global warming? Basically it is the planet heating up. The 1990s were the hottest decade of the last century and scientists say temperatures could rise by up to another 8°C over the next 100 years. This is thought to be at least partly due to rising levels of carbon dioxide, a greenhouse gas generated by burning fossil fuels such as coal and petroleum (used to make petrol). Greenhouse gases trap the sun's heat by acting like a huge blanket.

This temperature rise could mean more droughts in some areas, flooding in other areas, higher sea levels and more frequent storms. The ice caps could melt and flood low-lying countries such as The Netherlands.

Politicians tend to focus on what will win them votes in six months' time, not what the world will be like in 20 or 30 years, so what can we do?

Last weekend I chaired the first Youth Environment Conference in Birmingham. More than 170 fourteen- to twenty-five-year-olds turned up for the debate and had the chance to question a panel of politicians.

One of the concerns was the use of fossil fuels for cars and generating electricity. Other concerns were the lack of green alternatives such as wind power or hydro-electric power, and the lack of recycling schemes.

But what concerned us most was how we can make a difference. Lots of people don't understand what's happening to the planet so we need to show how important the environment is. If enough people think about this when they vote, then politicians will start to take note. Many of them don't think anybody cares and the only way we'll get them to do something is by demonstrating that we do care.

HOTTING UP: The first Youth Environment Conference put pressure on politicians

T2, The Daily Telegraph

5b Answer true (T) or false (F).

1   The article was written by a professional journalist. ...*F*...
2   The environment has been an important issue recently. .....
3   The end of the 20th century was hotter than the beginning. .....
4   Scientists think that the 21st century will not be as hot as the 20th century. .....
5   The level of carbon dioxide in the air is increasing. .....
6   Because of the greenhouse effect, everywhere will have more rain. .....
7   In the writer's opinion, politicians care about the long-term future of the Earth. .....
8   The writer had an important role at the Youth Environment Conference. .....
9   The Youth Environment Conference was for people of any age. .....
10 The most important issue of the conference was how to create alternative sources of energy. .....

5c Read the article again and underline the words and phrases connected with the environment. Then put them into the following groups.

Pollution
global warming, ...

Weather conditions
....

Effects on the environment
....

Fuel	Green energy	Other environmentally friendly ideas
....	....	....
....	....	....

6 Write ten words and five expressions you are going to memorize.

Words		Expressions	
1	1	....	
2		....	
3	2	....	
4		....	
5	3	....	
6		....	
7	4	....	
8		....	
9	5	....	
10		....	

Test yourself 3 (Units 9 to 12)

How much can you remember?

My mark: _____
60

1 Answer the questions.

What kind of artist are they?

0	I make things out of clay and porcelain.	*a ceramicist*
1	I paint.	....
2	I take photos.	....
3	I make things out of wood and marble.	....
4	I do drawings for books.	....

What kind of writer are they?

0	I write books about people's lives.	*a biographer*
5	I write novels.	....
6	I write poems.	....
7	I write plays.	....
8	I write for a newspaper about cars.	....
9	I write for a newspaper about the best things to buy.	....
10	I write for a newspaper about other countries' affairs.	....

(10 marks)

2 Name

five more things a painter might use:

a sketch pad .... , ... , ... , ...
, ... , ...

three more works of art a painter might produce:

a watercolour .... , ... , ... , ...

two more things a photographer might use:

a dark room .... , ... , ...

(10 marks)

3 Complete this film review.

Steven Spielberg's *Minority Report* is
⁰ *based* .... on a book by Philip K
Dick which is a both a ¹sc............-
fiction novel and a ²thr................ .
    The film is ³ s.....................
in Washington DC. The main
⁴ ch...................., played by Tom
Cruise, is head of the Pre-Crime Unit,
whose job is to stop crime before it
happens. The action takes place in
the future, but it is rooted in the
present. The main ⁵th.............. of
the film is the price we have to pay
for our liberty.

(5 marks)

4 Name ten sections of a newspaper.

0 *the travel section* .....

1 ....

2 ....

3 ....

4 ....

5 ....

6 ....

7 ....

8 ....

9 ....

10 ....

(10 marks)

5 Complete the sentences.

1 A play is divided into *acts*.............. and ....

2 A novel is divided into ....

3 A poem is divided into ....

4 A small-format newspaper is called a ....

5 A children's cartoon newspaper is a ....

6 A .... magazine tells you which films are on.

7 A .... magazine appears every week.

8 Critics write .... of films or books.

9 An .... gives the editor's opinions.

(9 marks)

6 Complete the conversation.

Joe: I'm bored with all this talk about the greenhouse ⁰*effect*..........., global ¹.................... , acid ².................... and the hole in the ozone ³....................

Emma: You might be bored with it, but it's happening.

Joe: I know, but what can I do about toxic ⁴.................... and the ⁵.................... of the rainforest? I'm not going to feel guilty about it.

Emma: Well, we've got to do something. We've got to look at alternative ⁶.................... of energy, like solar ⁷...................., and we've got to build more wind ⁸.................... We can't go on using ⁹.................... fuels like coal.

Joe: OK, OK, but what can I do?

Emma: You could join a pressure ¹⁰....................

Joe: You mean, become an ¹¹ eco-...................! No, thanks!

Emma: Well you can do small things, like ¹².................... paper and glass.

Joe: I already do.

Emma: And you cycle to college.

Joe: Yes, and I breathe in all the exhaust ¹³.................... ! I can't wait till we have solar-powered cars rather than ones that use ¹⁴.................... or ¹⁵.................... for fuel.

Emma: There you are. You're already an ¹⁶.................... campaigner!

(16 marks)

Reference

Jobs

See Unit 3, The business world, pages 18 – 19.

Generic terms

manager	assistant
project manager	clerk
consultant	secretary
officer	receptionist
advisor	worker /
supervisor	(machine) operator

See also People at work, page 18.

There are hundreds of job titles. Here is a selection.

Banking and accountancy

accountant	bank manager
accounts manager	bank clerk

Building and engineering

architect	surveyor
civil / mechanical / electrical / chemical engineer	town planner

Childcare

childminder	nursery nurse

Construction and building maintenance

builder	painter and decorator
carpenter	plumber
heating engineer	

Customer services

call centre agent / operator

Food preparation

baker	fishmonger
butcher	

Health

dentist	optician
general practitioner / doctor	paramedic
nurse	physiotherapist
	surgeon

Hotels and restaurants

chef	hotel receptionist
cook	waiter, waitress
hotel porter	

Housing

estate agent

Information technology

computer engineer
computer programmer
software engineer

Law

See Unit 8, The law and crime, page 50.

Media

See Unit 9, Newspapers and magazines, page 58.

Public services

firefighter	road sweeper
librarian	social worker
police officer	youth and community worker
postal worker	
prison officer	
refuse collector	

Science

chemist
laboratory technician
research scientist

Shops

cashier
shopkeeper
shop assistant

Telecommunications

telephone engineer
TV, video and audio engineers

Transport and vehicle maintenance

airline pilot	(motor) mechanic
bus conductor	taxi / cab driver
bus driver	van driver

The British government

See Unit 7, *People and politics*, page 44.

Assembly	Upper House	Lower House
Parliament (England)	The House of Lords	The House of Commons
The Scottish Parliament	–	–
The Welsh Assembly	–	–

The **Prime Minister** is the head of government. He or she chooses a group of about 20 ministers, known as the '**Cabinet**', to decide government policy. Members of the Cabinet include the Chancellor of the Exchequer (responsible for finance), the Home Secretary (responsible for 'home affairs', such as policing and prisons) and the Foreign Secretary.

Members of Parliament (MPs) sit in the **House of Commons**. There are 651 MPs in the House of Commons. The Scottish Parliament has 129 MSPs (Members of the Scottish Parliament).

Members of Parliament are elected by the people. They make the laws of the land by debating issues of current concern, like health and education, and proposing **Bills** which, if approved, are passed as Acts of Parliament. **Elections** are held every five years, although the Prime Minister may decide to call an election early.

There are about 700 **Lords**. They are not elected by the people. Most are appointed as a reward for public service. Some members of the Church of England also sit in the Lords.

One of the main functions of the **House of Lords** is to examine and revise Bills proposed by the House of Commons.

Main political parties in Britain

Conservative ('Tory')
Liberal Democrat
Labour

He's a	Conservative.
	Liberal Democrat.
	Labour voter.
	member of the … party.

Other parties include the Greens; the Scottish Nationalists; and, in Northern Ireland, the Ulster Unionists, the Social Democratic and Labour Party, and Sinn Fein.

The US government

Congress is the name given to the institution elected to make laws in the US. It consists of the Senate and the House of Representatives.

The Senate is composed of 100 members – two from each state. They must be at least 30 years old. Senators are elected every six years.

There are 435 members of the House of Representatives. They must be at least 25 years old and they are elected every two years.

The two main parties in Congress are the Democrats and the Republicans. Presidential elections take place every four years.

The legal system in the United States

See Unit 8, *The law and crime*, page 50.

State Courts deal with cases against the laws of a particular state. Federal Courts deal with cases against the laws of the United States as a whole or with crimes that cross state lines.

Accused people found guilty in a State or County Court have the right to appeal to an Appellate Court, and then a State Supreme Court. Accused people found guilty in a federal District Court have the right to appeal to a Court of Appeals. They do not have a right to be heard by the Supreme Court, which decides which cases it will hear.

British and American English

British	American
1 People and relationships (See page 6.)	
straight	straightforward
get on with	get along with
fall out with	break up with
be keen on	be interested in
fancy	like
Are you in a relationship at the moment?	Are you in a relationship right now?
move house	move
2 Everyday life (See page 12.)	
a heap of rubbish	a pile of trash
a joint of meat	a roast / (name of cut, e.g. a leg of lamb)
a bar of chocolate	a candy / chocolate bar
a lump of butter	a pat of butter
3 The business world (See page 18.)	
industrial estate	industrial park
workmate (in a factory)	co-worker
member of a trade union	member of a labor union
accounts (department)	accounting (department)
job advertisement / advert	help wanted ad
When are you available for interview?	When are you available for an interview?
He was sacked. / He got the sack.	He was fired. / He got fired.
He was made redundant.	He was laid off.
They've gone on strike.	They went on strike / were on strike.
4 Travelling and working abroad (See page 24.)	
take a year out / a gap year	take a year off
go trekking	go hiking / go backpacking
I got sponsorship from several local companies.	Several local companies sponsored me.

British	American
voluntary work	volunteer work
training course	(computer / proofreading) course / class
community work	volunteer work in a foreign country
adventure project	no equivalent
Is the work paid or is it voluntary?	Is this a job or volunteer work?
5 Looking after the body (See page 32.)	
vitamins	pronunciation: 'vytaminz'
fibre	spelling: fiber
have a shower	take a shower
have a wash	wash up
clean / brush your teeth	brush your teeth
cotton wool	cotton ball
washbag	toiletry kit / shaving kit (for men) / makeup bag (for women)
be / feel poorly	be / feel sick / ill / bad
be fit and healthy	be in (good) shape
have (got) a fever	have a fever
have (got) ... asthma, etc.	have asthma, etc.
complementary medicine	no equivalent
go into hospital	go into the hospital
take tablets	take pills
have physiotherapy	have physical therapy
6 Society (See page 38.)	
(family) gathering	family reunion (organized event, infrequent); family get-together (casual)
I'm in a (football) team.	I'm on a (football) team.
(local history) society	(local historical) society
7 People and politics (See page 44. Also see Reference, page 85, for information about the British and US governments.)	
the opposition	no equivalent
a coalition government	no equivalent

British	American	British	American
Member of Parliament (MP)	Member of Congress; Senator, Congress-man / woman	He got a life sentence.	He was committed for life. / He was committed for a life term.
government minister	Secretary of (Defense, Treasury, etc.)	He went down for three years.	He was sent up for three years. / He went away for three years. / He did three years.
councillor	councilman / woman		
in the centre	middle of the road	He got done for robbery.	*no equivalent*
centre-left / left of centre	liberal		

9 Newspapers and magazines (See page 58.)

British	American
centre-right / right of centre	conservative
run / stand for Parliament	run for office; *colloquial:* 'to throw one's hat in the ring'
floating voter	independent / undeclared voter
general election	primary election; general election = presidential / congressional election

British	American
comic	comic book
listings magazine	'what's on' magazine; events guide /calendar
a fortnightly magazine	a bimonthly magazine
social affairs	society / fashion and style
motoring	automotive
home news	national news
world news	international news
editorial or leader	editorial
advert	advertisement / ad / classified section

8 The law and crime (See page 50. Also see Reference, page 85 for information about the US system.)

British	American
a barrister / solicitor	lawyer / attorney / counselor
chairman of the jury	presiding juror / jury foreperson
the defence	*spelling:* the defense
fraudster	conman
He was sent for trial.	*no equivalent*
His neighbours gave evidence against him.	His neighbors testified against him.
licence	*spelling:* license
He was banned from driving for two years.	His driving privileges were suspended for two years.
He's now got a criminal record.	He has a criminal record.
He did 100 hours of community service.	He performed 100 hours of community service.
He went to a young offenders' institution.	He went to a youth offender program. / He went to the youth authority.

10 Books (See page 64.)

British	American
dialogue	*spelling:* dialog
I read it in translation.	I read a translation.

11 Art (See page 70.)

British	American
a watercolour	*spelling:* a watercolor
film (*countable in BrE*)	rolls of film

12 The environment (See page 76.)

British	American
petrol	gasoline
fertilisers	*spelling:* fertilizers
eco-warrior	ecology activist

Bye!

USA

Self assessment and progress check

Self assessment

Fill in the chart when you have completed each unit.

	Which vocabulary sections were the most useful? (e.g. Friendships and relationships)	How well did you do in the exercises? very | quite | not so well Tick the correct part of the line.	You wrote down some words and expressions to memorize. How many of them can you remember? Words /10 Expressions /5	Which vocabulary sections do you need to go over again before you do the test?
1 People and relationships		▬▬▬		
2 Everyday life		▬▬▬		
3 The business world		▬▬▬		
4 Travelling and working abroad		▬▬▬		

Test score: / 60

5 Looking after the body		▬▬▬		
6 Society		▬▬▬		
7 People and politics		▬▬▬		
8 The law and crime		▬▬▬		

Test score: / 60

9 Newspapers and magazines		▬▬▬		
10 Books		▬▬▬		
11 Art		▬▬▬		
12 The environment		▬▬▬		

Test score: / 60

Progress check

How much of the vocabulary did you know **before** you worked through the units?
How much do you feel you know **after** working through the units?

		Less than 25%	About 50%	More than 60%
Units 1 – 4	before			
	after			
Units 5 – 8	before			
	after			
Units 9 – 12	before			
	after			